OVER THE TRANSOM

CONFESSIONS OF A WANNABE WRITER

BY

THOMAS LYNN

SOUTHERN CHARM PRESS

Printed and bound in the United States of America. All rights reserved. No part of this book may be reproduced or transmitted in any form or by any means, electronic or mechanical, including photocopying, recording, or by information storage and retrieval system—except by a reviewer who may quote brief passages in a review to be printed in a magazine or newspaper. For information, please contact Southern Charm Press, 150 Caldwell Drive, Hampton, Georgia 30228.

Copyright © 2002 by Thomas Lynn

All rights reserved.
Southern Charm Press, 150 Caldwell Drive, Hampton, GA 30228
Visit our Web site at www.southerncharmpress.com

The publisher offers discounts on this book when purchased in quantities. For more information, contact: toll free: 1-888-281-9393, fax: 770-946-5220, e-mail: info@southerncharmpress.com

Printed in the United States of America
First Printing: October 2002

Library of Congress Control Number
      LCCN: 2001096444

Lynn, Thomas
Over The Transom:
Confessions of a Wannabe Writer / Thomas Lynn

      ISBN 0-9714832-9-9

Cover design by Ariana Overton of Cover Art By Ariana

OVER THE TRANSOM

CONFESSIONS OF A WANNABE WRITER

BY

THOMAS LYNN

This book is dedicated to my mother
Mary Frances Lynn

FOREWORD

Step inside Thomas Lynn's childhood memories and indulge yourself in his rich descriptions of early days and his burning ambition to write. He fulfilled his ambition and his pen often jousted with the likes of William Shakespeare, Thomas Moore and Limrik, of whom the last may not be familiar to you — yet. With vivid description, Lynn leads his readers into the beginning of rhyme with Limrik back in the Pliocene, catapults us into Will Rogers' gentle humor and teaches us to appreciate the poet Shelley. No matter the topic or genre, Lynn fearlessly attacks his topic with tongue glued to his cheek and fingers dancing over his computer keyboard. Read on for adventure, humor and thrills, but be warned: Tom Lynn avoids sex, politics and religion, to jaded readers' relief. I am pleased to offer his latest work to his fans.

— *Linda Hutton*
Editor, Rhyme Time and Mystery Time

PREFACE

Wannabe writers are unknown in the literary field. No one has ever heard of them and they are not represented by agents. Their manuscripts are usually submitted to publishers over the transom; that is, submitted without being specifically requested. It seems that everybody today wants to write poems, song lyrics, essays, magazine articles, books, and biographies.

People have suddenly leaped up as if they were touched with an electric prod to proclaim, "I want to be a writer!"

From where did this urge originate? Did someone start spreading the news that there is a lot of money in being a writer? Pity the poor soul who believes such fantasy for he is certainly headed down the garden path toward frustration and disillusionment. For every beginning writer who actually succeeds in seeing his byline published on a regular basis, uncounted others are standing in the wings awaiting their big break. One doesn't become a writer overnight and if everyone who ever wanted to be a writer were placed end to end, the line would probably stretch from O. Henry to Hemingway and back again.

The experiences of aspiring and successful writers alike are similar and often amusing to share. We all have to start someplace and just so there is no misunderstanding about what beginners can expect in their climb upward, I have compiled many of my own published articles and essays into an informal guide for new writers. They were carefully chosen and presented here to help smooth the pathways ahead and to make things easier for the wannabe who decides to step out onto that avenue of dreams.

Believable or not, the chapters of this book are filled with whimsical absurdities intermingled with truly serious lessons to be learned as readers are introduced to Limrik (the caveman poet), Honey Bun Singletary (everyone's sweetheart), Wilbur Lovelylocks (proprietor of Ye Olde Poetry Shoppe) and Henry Wadsworth Matsumoto (writer's club president). We will whimsically delve together into the literary minds of Edgar Allan Poe and William Shakespeare.

So sit back, relax, and prepare to enjoy what follows. If others wish to join us, they are also welcome for all who enjoy writing are certain to come away with a smile or chuckle at some of the personal drolleries and outlandish shaggy tales told on these pages.

At least, such is my fondest hope.

CHAPTER ONE

Let me confess at the outset that I didn't *always* want to be a writer myself. I remember an early fascination for ten-gallon cowboy hats, leather chaps, and pearl-handled six guns. Afterwards came a yearning to be a baseball player for the St. Louis Browns. It was a lofty ambition at the time — my hero was Chet Laabs (look him up). I might have settled for the life of a soldier with a tin helmet, uniform with shiny brass buttons, and no one to mind if face and hands got dirty. Later, of course, I was a super hero with my own homemade cape, leaping from the garage roof to apprehend imaginary bad guys. My desire to be a writer started sometime between first grade and long trousers.

Growing up in south St. Louis during the Depression years of the thirties was traumatic enough without broadcasting to all my playtime friends that I yearned to be a writer some day. It just wasn't done.

"Hey, Spike! Where's Eddie?"

"Dunno, 'cept he might still be at home."

"At home? What's so important that he can't be here with the rest of the guys? We got stuff to do today."

Someone would surely have blown the whistle on me. "Nah, he's prob'ly at the liberry writing some kind of story. He's been doing a lot of that lately." I can imagine Spike rolling his eyes in disgust and shaking his head in disbelief that anyone would rather be doing *that* than skipping rocks or other important guy things.

Memory recalls that the impetus to write probably began with a youthful Valentine's Day shopping tour at Kresge's 5&10. It was the most popular store in my neighborhood but I was disappointed at the Valentine cards on display. They were various shapes and sizes with hearts and Cupid's arrows and covered with mushy-gushy love offerings.

"Be Mine!" they proclaimed.

"You're My Valentine!"

"Our Hearts Shall Beat As One!"

What a bunch of twaddle. Who wrote all that icky stuff anyway? I could write better verses than that. As usual, it was my mother who selected all the cards for me to give my little friends. I washed my hands of the whole deal. She addressed the envelopes and signed my name inside each card while I retired to my bedroom, first to sulk and then to create my own Valentines with more appropriate sentiments.

To my teacher I wrote, *Miss Brown, you're so round. Your big old feet pound holes in the ground but I really can say on this Valentine's Day that you're not the worst teacher I've found.* Personally, I thought that was pretty good but Mother absolutely refused to let me mail it. Likewise, none of my other creative verses passed her inspection.

It was my first editorial rejection.

There would be others.

Many people wonder what the great fascination is in becoming a writer. I can only answer that unlike others who profess to have an unquenchable hunger to devise artistic creations of purest poetry, my motives were quite basic. I was simply intrigued with the lyrical tones of certain words and phrases that I found in the lines of Wordsworth, Tennyson and Longfellow. Furthermore, there didn't seem to be much hard manual labor involved.

I didn't realize it but my very young brain was having its initial encounter with rhyme and rhythm. Alliteration and assonance loomed on the horizon and I reached hungrily for other poetic phenomena while simultaneously exploring the fluid motion of storytelling. I have since discovered that the road traveled by writers is an arduous one but being an avid reader was a definite asset in my quest for literary success.

Robert Louis Stevenson and Edgar Allan Poe were among my early heroes but I later enjoyed Zane Grey and James Thurber as well. It wasn't the finished product of these writers that held my interest as much as the different approaches in their development of characters, dialogue and plot. I compared the methods of various other novelists and essayists and soon learned that although good writers were also good poets, it didn't necessarily follow that all poets were good writers.

I found that poetry was decidedly evident in the works of the best writers from all eras. In fact, many of their writings were sufficiently lyrical as to be sung. I need only point out the Irish lilt of Thomas Moore.

***

Believe me if all those endearing young charms
Which I gaze on so fondly today,
Were to change by tomorrow, and fleet in my arms
Like fairy-gifts fading away!
Then would'st still be adored, as this moment thou art,
Let thy loveliness fade as it will,
And around the dear ruin each wish of my heart
Would entwine itself verdantly still...

***

Such were the qualities I wished to emulate and over the years it became more apparent that being an accomplished writer was akin to being a poet and a lyricist. Consequently, despite the modest number of publishing credits I have earned since the days of ducking Spike and the guys, it is still my desire to become a noted writer, some day.

I don't think Spike would understand.

CHAPTER TWO

Cowboys are the natural heroes of all young boys. Riding the range, roping dogies, eating beans from a frying pan like Tom Mix, Buck Jones, or Hopalong Cassidy. It's an ideal life. My best friend Bobby Wierock wanted to be a fireman but I thought that was silly. It might have been fun to hang onto the side of a big red fire truck complete with ladders and hoses and a loud clanging bell, but firemen are always washing and polishing those big trucks. You can bet Tom Mix never washed and polished his horse.

My childhood years included an abundance of playtime but there was a bit of poetry here and there. My mother loved poetry. She often read to me from a small book of verse. Its cover was tattered and frayed and some of the pages peeked out with bravery but she read aloud and I thrilled to the stories she told. Of course I didn't know she was reading poetry because the words hardly ever rhymed and she seldom paused at line endings, continuing to read as she would an adventure tale. My imagination stirred to hear her recitation and the words came alive for that brief moment. I longed for the ability to put words together like that.

A certain aura of glamour has always been associated with being a poet and a writer that belies its laborious nature. Much later came the realization that writing is hard work and not at all as I envisioned it. Scintillating words and phrases never flowed effortlessly from the recesses of my brain. Composing stirring accounts of life, without pause for breath, was not really my forte and the postman seldom delivered weekly royalty checks to my front door. The thrill of writing erupted whenever my manuscript reached the climax of another mystery adventure. Then I was borne from this temporal world, not to return until a new sheet of paper found its way into that old Underwood and another Chapter One began.

    I must admit that I have become accustomed to certain advantages of the writing profession and I rather enjoy my freedom from the rigors of menial toil that often makes the average person irritable, sweaty and fatigued beyond decency. It's true I don't smoke a pipe but I do own a dog and a fireplace and on cold wintry evenings I sip hot chocolate and skim the New York Times bestseller list. It wasn't always this good, however. There were moments that tried the marrow of my creative spirit. It was especially so in the beginning.

    During my sophomore year at Herculaneum High School I had a serious crush on Miss Higgins, my English teacher, until she announced her upcoming marriage. I was heartbroken. Naturally her betrothal removed any incentive I may have had to become a novelist and I channeled all my unrequited energy into playing second base for the Herky High Black Cats. Unfortunately, during our opening game I struck out four times and lost my place on the team to Fat Pat Fribley. She was a freshman.

    Unlucky in love and sports I was barely able to maintain a low profile in school until final exam week. We were assigned to write a poem in the style of Edgar Allan Poe. Strangely enough, Poe was one of my favorites. I could readily identify with him because of our mutual fondness for old clocks and black birds.

    I screened all interruptions from mind as my pencil raced across the test paper. Perhaps old Edgar himself guided my hand for the poem seemed to create itself. I allowed the hypnotic verse to etch itself into my memory, then with supreme confidence I strode to Miss Higgins' desk and presented my masterpiece. She smiled but I shrugged it off with indifference. The torch had burned out.

    Patience was never my greatest virtue but I managed to contain myself the next morning as I awaited the test results. Soon I would be able to hold my head up high, to scoff at love's capricious whims, to play second base again.

"Class", Miss Higgins rapped a pencil on her desk to gain attention. "I was pleased with the results of yesterday's examination. You were all quite good and I am proud of each one of you."

Why didn't she get on with it?

"There was one poem in particular that I must share with you."

I knew she would be impressed.

"This is one of the finest poetic compositions I have ever read by a high school student. It is titled 'Portrait Of Lenore' and was written by our own Honey Bun Singletary."

I was devastated! Surely there was some mistake. Did she not read my poem? From far away I heard her discussing it. "Special mention for his satiric wit . . . burlesque and parody."

Because of that traumatic experience I never became a distinguished author or a famous poet. I have since consoled myself with the words of Walt Whitman who put it quite succinctly. "To have great poetry," he said, "there must be great audiences." Miss Higgins was just not that great an audience. My biggest regret though was I never again played second base for the Herky Black Cats.

Sorrow is often forgotten with the passage of time and in due course I rediscovered the fascination of literature. Books especially, with their orderly pages and colorful pictures. Reading again became one of the true pleasures of my life. Baseball, girls and pickup trucks competed for second place in importance. Other young boys longed to imitate Tom Sawyer and cringed in delightful terror at the evils of Dr. Jekyll and Mr. Hyde while my heroes were their creators. I often imagined myself living in the eras of Mark Twain and Robert Louis Stevenson, sitting on a wooden stool, holding a long plumed pen in my hand and confidently composing a novel of unquestioned immortality.

Today, I am a few years older. Apart from the wrinkles that line my face or the grandchildren clamoring at my knee, my unfulfilled ambition of becoming a famed novelist has not diminished. It may have been temporarily set aside due to certain necessary changes in my schedule of priorities, but it yet lingers. If it had remained atop my list I might have created an unforgettable love story or a chilling murder mystery, but I never found the time to write that bestseller.

Even now in the quiet of the evening when the family has settled down in slumber and the house itself seems to relax with an audible sigh, I lay awake and wonder how different my life would be if I had written that book.

In the realm of pretense I would have planned my fictional characters, devised living personalities and had them overcome many adversities in their literary travails. I would have spent many hours in solitude perfecting every paragraph and chapter. The aspirations and heroic deeds of my protagonist would have been vividly and graphically depicted. My clever resolution of calamitous situations would certainly have enthralled faithful readers and they would have been unable to put my novel down until digesting it in its entirety. My novel would have reposed atop the New York Times list and Universal Studios would have offered a fortune for movie rights. Letterman would be pleading for my appearance, Norman Mailer would now be a bosom pal and my wife would have probably filed for divorce before moving to Honolulu with my grandchildren, my royalties, and my dog.

If I had written that book, I would be visiting libraries and book fairs to autograph each copy purchased by adoring fans. The young ladies would have been captivated by my charm as I inscribed a personal memento on the flyleaf. I would have heartily shaken hands with the old men while listening graciously as little old ladies shyly asked, "Do you think sex and violence are really necessary in a best-selling novel?" And I would wink and observe their rosy blushes at my teasing reply. "Of course not . . . but it does put the author in a favorable mood to write one."

CHAPTER THREE

The greatest fallacy in being a writer is believing that happiness lies in the actual act of writing. It does not. Happiness only comes when the writing is completed. Whether the tools are pen or computer, writers always begin their work with little more than an idea and words must somehow find their way onto paper or monitor screen. Beginning is the worst part. Middles and endings eventually follow but it is the beginning that kicks the whole thing off. Far be it for me, an aspirant myself, to introduce disillusionment to the dreamers who envision themselves basking in the glory of literary fame and royalties but writing is really the most difficult of human experiences. It's a heart-wrenching, soul-searching, mind-boggling task that brings pleasure only when it is over and the writer is then able to breathe a sigh of relief as the finished manuscript wings its way around the publishing circuit.

The exact day and hour in which I first seriously began to string words together is difficult to pinpoint. I vaguely recall an original little verse that I recited as a youngster. In those days it was customary on the night before Halloween, we called it *all beggar's night,* for children to costume themselves as clowns or witches and visit neighbors to perform something appropriate as an inducement for candy treats. Failure to provide a suitable ransom was sufficient motive for revenge on the following night. I couldn't sing or dance so I usually wore a jester's hat and entertained with this ditty.

"I know a little song. It ain't very long.

Toodle-up, Toodle-up, now it's all gone."

My obvious embarrassment at such unaccustomed once-a-year performances usually resulted in chocolate kisses, red hots, or jawbreakers and may have been the catalyst for literary creations in subsequent years. The candy treats have since become bylines and occasionally, even checks.

Sometimes there is a great compulsion for the writer to explain why he has chosen to write. Time and again trade publications solicit articles on the subject. Beginners scramble to produce appropriate answers because they sense a possible byline, and professional writers who have striven long in their craft without great financial reward, often fall victim in a sense of nostalgia to expound on their reasons for being what they are or rather, what they would like to be.

As often as not, a writer has no true insight into his motives. Perhaps he writes to express himself or as an attempt to achieve some sort of immortality by use of the written word. Few will admit they seek an easy path to fortune, a path that has excluded physical exertion or mental stress. It is a rare person who devotes his lifetime to the development of prose or poetry out of sheer fascination for the science of language. Yet, that is the absolute rationalization.

Magazines and trade journals that sponsor the submission of essays on this topic do so from a need to fill their pages rather than from any great desire to provide a service to the writing community. Publishers fail to understand that writers do not really care why others write; they know only their own hunger.

Ours is a craft that unfortunately is obsessed with itself. Its members appear at times to perform more for the acclamation of each other than for the benefit of readers. This is evident from writings in which writers clearly call out to each other, "Look! I have fathered another creation!" The domino effect then demands a counter product to demonstrate that other writers have kept pace. The result is a pompous assembly line of pretentious drivel that is of interest only to other equally insincere writers.

"Why then," I ask myself, "why have I wanted to be a writer?" I suppose I became enamored with it after discovering that my most productive moments occurred while sitting. I never considered the likely possibility of drilling for oil, forging steel or delivering mail because each of these prospects require a lot of standing and very little sitting. Sitting jobs, undoubtedly the hereditary result of a long line of professional sitters, has eternally fascinated me.

History fails to mention it but this peculiar family trait was first evidenced by my great-great-great-great grandfather who was responsible for the famous ride of Paul Revere in 1775. It seems that Grandpa was relaxing as usual in his favorite rocking chair when he heard thundering hoof beats fast approaching. He recognized the bellowing of that pesky Revere fellow and, as the horseman paused in the darkness to complain loudly about red coats, Gramps tossed a handful of China Red firecrackers at the horse's feet. As the rider galloped wildly out of town he was heard to remark about Grandpa's suspected illicit parentage. However, history does show that Paul Revere completed his journey in record time.

My own penchant for sitting should not falsely imply that I am athletically deficient. On the contrary, during my tenure at Herky High I nearly broke the state record for endurance squatting. It should not be surprising therefore that today finds me sitting at my desk, tenderly caressing my keyboard while another little verse breathes of life. Here, there is no time clock to punch, no machinery to clang, no production quota to maintain and, for all the reader knows, I am sitting here naked as a jaybird. The point is, I *am* sitting here and making little white lies seem real, so I suppose that is the primary reason I chose to be a writer.

Another word for it might be "imagination."

Imagination and creativity go hand in hand. Where you find one, you also find the other. For instance, when did the art of writing originate and who was the very first writer? Could it have been at some time and by someone before the advent of recorded history? In other words ⎯ prehistoric? This is where imagination takes over.

For example, it would truly have been a joyous occasion in those olden days. Singly and in pairs, they traveled long distances from the great ocean-sea, across the highlands of rugged crag and jutting tor to the gentle sloping hillside and familiar cavern of times long past. Imagine the tales they told around the old campfire — the lies, the romances, the beer. I'm sure there was a fight or two as new wives were introduced and old jealousies recalled. It was a once-in-a-lifetime event.

What a great bunch!

"Grock!" said Og the hunter, which was caveman talk for, "Please pass the gnu." As he speared a hefty drumstick, he would again exclaim, "Grock!" or "Hey, do you all remember the time when we . . ." and then would follow a narrative consisting of hilarious details surrounding a particularly perilous or sordid adventure augmented by lusty laughter as each contributed to the telling.

Who among them would ever forget the thrumming of tribal drums welcoming Rodag's triumphant return from the Wilderness as he held aloft the gleaming tusk of Sho-Tei, the great Mamut? There were remembrances of the courageous Tuleg who dared to eat the first chicken egg, and Limrik who seldom accompanied the clan on hunts but preferred instead to remain behind and carve pictures on the walls of the cave.

"Grock!" someone would cry and everyone would tease Limrik because of his penchant for sculpting the nudeness of heroic figures on the wall near his private resting place and then further embellishing them with catchy little five-line verses of impudent rhyme.

They were all there. The old gang . . . together again. Clag, Krubnik, and Thajanec from the fire brigade. Schultz the Outlander, as well as Mug and Pug, the Neanderthal twins. The campfire unquestionably burned late into the night and the cave echoed with raucous tales of adventure and epic conquests.

Fond reminiscences were exchanged about Jakalar. He was their leader who perished in the time of the ground-shaking when the valley opened its floor to smoke and the burning rocks. Jakalar was swallowed up by the chasm, never to be seen again and that was really when the tribe began to drift away and to pursue separate paths.

Fire shadows eerily danced upon the walls of that tribal cave as memories began to wane and it was time for the party to break up.

"Grock!" Clag said. His meaning was clear. "No more beer for me, guys. It's been a long day and I'm gonna turn in." He yawned loudly and stretched out in a darkened corner. They would all follow, one by one, until the far reaches of the cave filled with the sonorous slumbering of men pleased with their fill of gnu and strong drink.

Serenity prevailed and all was right with their world.

The members of the gathering were content with happy dreams of individual successes since leaving the clan. Tuleg had gone on to fame and fortune as inventor of the wheel and the thousand-mile checkup, while Mug and Pug started a rock group billed as, what else, The Rolling Stones. Clag went into real estate and Thajanec was saving souls while keeping one step ahead of the law in his new calling as an evangelist. Schultz ran a summer camp for wayward girls and Og became a football player for the Piltdown Boulders.

But it was Limrik who caused the biggest stir around that campfire. It was he of the satirical chisel for whom old friends convened to pay homage. Limrik, the Pliocene artiste, whose irreverent etchings and saucy rhymes catapulted him to the bestseller list and made his name a household word for all time.

"Grock!" said he in caveman language meaning, "If you got it, flaunt it."

Literary experts have long recognized the emergent genius of this man whose work survived lava flows, glacial eras, and the uplifting of whole continents. His intact cave carvings and reconstructed stone engravings offer proof that man's earliest ancestors were not only highly intelligent but also possessors of a humorous imagination. What other conclusion may be drawn from writings that call comical attention to modern preoccupations with human sexual appetites except . . . it has always been so.

One of Limrik's most ancient verses tells it best.

There was an old fossil from Kent

Who wedded young Oola from Ghent
He said with a smile,
It's been a long while —
I hope that my coming ain't went

"Grock!" which is caveman talk for, "I don't believe I'd have told that."

Seeing this as an example of how imagination leads to creativity, is it any wonder why I almost always wanted to be a writer?

CHAPTER FOUR

Essayists should possess a good sense of humor, but of more importance is their talent for fabricating falsehoods, in a controlled environment of course.

For instance; there's a cake on the kitchen table, one of those fancy kinds with an ice cream center and nuts and candles on the top. It's a birthday cake but I'm not going to say how many candles there are because it's *my* birthday. The only thing I can say is that if all those candles are lit at one time, the Lawrenceville Volunteer Fire Department will work overtime tonight.

Every year about this same time I get to feeling sad and teary-eyed because . . . well, what good is a guy's birthday if his mother isn't with him? She was there on the first one and it isn't as if she had a good excuse, like being sick or on her honeymoon. She only lives in the next State. According to an article in the Modern Mothers Journal, mothers are staying away from their children's' birthdays in ever increasing numbers. Especially when the children reach their sixty-something birthday. It seems to be some sort of adverse ancestral symbolism.

Perhaps dinosauritis.

That may have been what killed off all the old Tyrannosauruses and Triceratopsus; their mothers absented themselves from parental duties when needed the most — on their children's' birthdays. What a disappointment! I can imagine how they must have felt. There they were, standing around with all their little dinosaur friends waiting to enjoy fresh treetop salads and gaily-wrapped presents but they weren't having any fun. Their mothers had abandoned them. Probably because they had grown too big and too old and they constituted evidence that the mothers themselves were bigger and older.

Modern mothers similarly dislike being reminded they are bigger and older than their offspring. They show this quite subtly by replacing birthday gifts with pristine cards saying, "Thinking of you." Let's face it; a sixty-something child needs more than that. He needs the same pat on the head and the same sage advice as when he was only seven. Oh! How important, those pats on the head! They are sometimes the difference between winning and losing, but more often the difference between giving up and trying harder. My mother gave outstanding pats on the head. They reached deep inside and turned my "what's the use's" into "I can do its."

I also received my share of motherly advice although it was often hardly recognizable as such. Mothers have a way of lulling you with a guilt trip before catching you off balance with their lesson of the day. "Eddie, how many times have I told you to wash your face and hands before dinner?"

"I'm sorry, Mother," I forgot.

"Remember son, cleanliness is next to Godliness."

"Yes, ma'am. I'll remember." That particular lesson was easily forgotten I suppose because to this day I haven't the least idea what cleanliness has to do with Godliness. Does God only love clean people? Or does it mean that Angels don't wear socks in heaven?

There must be some heavy training in motherhood school because my mother had something to teach me about everything, whether marbles, baseball, or kites. It's obvious that she attended many of the same courses as other mothers to whom I have been exposed. I used to have a best friend named Bobby. We were both ten years old and spent a lot of time at each other's home. It was often difficult to remember whose home it was because our mothers gave identical advice.

"You both have to eat all of your carrots. Remember those poor starving children in Ethiopia!" Now, how were those kids going to get any carrots if we ate them all up first?

Romance is not popular among younger boys. I was thirteen before receiving my first serious kiss. Her name was Marlene and one day after school we were playing together in her daddy's hay barn when she wrestled me down and gave me a big, long, wet smooch right there between the bales. I had heard about kisses like that and I jumped up and ran all the way home, crying. My mother met me at the front porch and from the tears and hay straws sticking to my clothes, she thought I had been fighting. I explained about Marlene and asked if I had to marry her. I didn't even have a job.

Mother dried my tears and told me to sit at the kitchen table. This was going to be our most serious discussion about sex. "Son," she said. "Kisses are like candy mints." I could relate to that. "They're sweet to the taste, but . . ." There was always a "but" somewhere in her lessons. "You shouldn't be greedy and eat them all at once because . . . then you won't have any for tomorrow." I wasn't getting the message. "Do you understand what I'm saying?"

"No, ma'am. I don't think so."

"Well, let me put it this way." I watched her lips compress tightly. "You are never to play in the hay again with Marlene Applegate or I'll take a switch to you. Do you hear me?"

"Yes, ma'am." I got that message.

"And I'll have a talk with that girl's mother." There must have been a high-level mothers conference that evening because Marlene refused to speak to me the rest of the school year. That was fine with me because I wasn't ready to get married anyway.

All my life I have tried to follow my mother's advice. I have been a good son, always washing my face and hands before dinner, eating all my carrots, and I haven't seen Marlene since High School. Meanwhile, there's that birthday cake with all the unlighted candles and: uh, oh, excuse me. There's the phone.

"Hello."

"Why, thank you mother. It's nice of you to remember."

"That's all right. I know you would be here if you could."

"What's that? Oh, yes. I guess we'll have a cake later. You know birthdays aren't that big a deal when you reach a certain age."

"No, of course not, Mother. I was referring to my age."

"Yes, I'll remember to wash before dinner."

"Well, I don't think we're gonna have carrots but . . . "

"Now, Mother. I haven't seen her in years."

"Yes, I'll be happy to have you visit for my next birthday, Mother." Somebody better put the Lawrenceville Volunteer Fire Department on standby.

Since my entering into adulthood and attempting to enter the field of writing, I have discovered that those early childhood days are a continuing source of writing ideas. Much has been said concerning the writer's eternal search for a fountainhead of marketable ideas. Articles, fiction and poetry normally follow each other in prolific profusion until the well runs dry. That's when a writer earns his meager wage.

Like other sufferers, I have tried many methods of surmounting that hurdle known as writer's block. One supposedly certain cure is the old relaxing trick. That's when the afflictee closes his eyes and erases everything from conscious thought. Some writers would probably not find this to be particularly difficult. However, the truth is that no matter how relaxed the mind may seem to be, the body knows otherwise and reacts differently as fingers twitch uncontrollably, straining to reach an imaginary keyboard.

A magazine article once suggested that this problem could be best overcome by copying a page or more from a published essay or short story in draft form as if writing it for editorial submission. The reasoning being that practice jogs the memory and causes creative juices to flow, putting words on paper, which is what a writer is supposed to do. Personally, I have an aversion to copying someone else's material and cannot help but wonder where that particular writer got his idea.

Postponing the problem by leaving one's work area for a brisk walk around the neighborhood is not a system that works very well either. For one thing it only produces antagonism toward whoever refuses to keep yapping dogs within required backyard confines. Who can concentrate with a Great Dane polo pony loudly protesting every step, or a hairy Tibetan chow gazing hungrily with yellow eyes? Some writers attack this disabling barrier by indulging in late night snacks. I have found, however, that the soothing of raveled nerves with coffee, warm milk, cold beer, a ham on rye, or Maalox usually promotes nothing more significant than a steadily increasing urge to visit that small porcelanized room upstairs.

The most worthwhile suggestion to come to my attention is to carry a notebook everywhere. I purchased a small one at Wal-Mart and the two of us became inseparable. We were as Damon and Pythias, bacon and eggs, rum and coke, etc. We were together at baseball games, church and movies. My notebook remained on my bedside table at night because it is common knowledge that many story ideas occur during sleep. My wife often remarked that I did my best work then but I have never fully understood her comment. I envisioned myself lying on the brink of somnolence, suddenly leaping to the floor with a bound and a cry of "Eureka!" followed by a frantic recording of the perfect rhyme for my ongoing epic or a masterful solution to a struggling murder mystery.

For weeks I dutifully positioned that notebook near at hand but not one single creative thought occurred as I lay in bed with my hands folded across my chest, waiting.

Once, I did bolt upright but the thought that struck me was more erotic than poetic. I mulled it over for several moments before deciding against writing it down. I was fearful that my wife might find it the next morning and either revile me for being a dirty old man or forever wonder if she had unknowingly slept through something during the night.

Walking in the woods can be fun especially when one is intuitively attuned to nature. Being the sensitive artist that I am means I am naturally on familiar terms with trees, daffodils and birds a-feather. I am also somewhat acquainted with mosquitoes, ants and black furry things that crawl up my pants leg without invitation.

It was on such an excursion that I found myself with other members of the Lawrenceville Poetry Club. Normally when I commune with flora and fauna, I prefer being alone. Not that I'm antisocial but flora and fauna often tend to make me sneeze, itch or yelp with acute pain and I would rather not share such moments with others. I was unaware of this scheduled field trip because I hadn't attended the last two meetings. It was the telephone call from Henry Wadsworth Matsumoto, our beloved club President that convinced me to stimulate my latent creativity in the company of my fellow versifiers. He threatened to have my Golden Poet Award recalled if I failed to show up.

So there I was in the deep piney forest harking to echoes of woodland nymphs and drinking in the beauty of the wild for the sake of poetry, and to retain my Golden Poet Award. I observed my fellow club members basking in the moment. Some with eyes shut in obvious rapture while others were busily recording imagistic sensations in their journals. I closed my own eyes several times to meditate only to sense the nearby presence of our President. He was apparently on guard to differentiate between meditation and slumber. Despite my strenuous efforts, inspiration evaded my desperate pleading and my pen remained idle.

True to my poetic calling, I bared my soul to the aura and testimony of Mother Nature. I even cheated somewhat by tightly squinting my eyes but the only message perceived was a tiny voice chanting as if from afar.

> *There is naught here for verse or poem,*
> *So get off my rock and go back home.*

I declined to write it down for fear that H.W.M would fail to understand the gravity of the situation. Nevertheless, by unanimous vote I was expelled at the next meeting due to my "uncooperative attitude." I was instructed to return my miniature penlight and autographed Walt Whitman portrait but was allowed to retain my official tee shirt and World Of Poetry coffee mug.

Being drummed out of the club was indeed humiliating and certainly not an experience to wish upon anyone. I thank my lucky stars that through it all I was able to salvage something of moderate value. Yes, on my bedroom wall there still hangs that proud symbol with which so many fortunates have been honored.

My coveted Golden Poet Award.

CHAPTER FIVE

I have yet to write the great American novel. It's on my agenda but I thought perhaps I should practice first on something easier, like a western. Yes! I could write a cowboy story. My hero would be Tex Laramie, a rugged outdoorsman with the strength of ten ordinary men. Tex would sit tall in the saddle and be the champion of the weak and downtrodden in the old west. On each hip would rest a Colt .44 revolver with which he could snuff a candle flame or an outlaw with either hand. He would ride a rangy sorrel named Wildfire and be equally adept at roping dogies or beautiful cowgirls.

Tex Laramie would wend his way across the pages of frontier history as a drover, Pony Express rider, Indian scout, and secret agent for Wells Fargo. Despite many harrowing adventures he would somehow manage to retain his boyhood charm and jovial good nature while simultaneously displaying exceptional talent for fairness and sound judgment. In all his escapades from Montana to the Rio Grande, Tex would always obey the unwritten code of the west. He would never draw first!

Writing western adventures, ala Louis Lamour is certainly more enjoyable than laboring over the growth of a classic novel. My cowboy protagonist could plunge right into action without the need for introductory chapters. The general tempo could be varied according to the number of pages anticipated in the storytelling and my hero could be involved in several perilous situations or in one continuing hazardous exploit consisting of lesser plights. I could introduce as many or as few characters as desired and they could speak in slangy dialogue or graphic metaphor. Additionally, my story plot could continue in either humorous or dramatic style from beginning to climax.

As I review the words written above there comes to mind a realization that the effort undertaken in writing western adventures is not at all unlike the drudgery of writing a novel. Perhaps I should practice writing something even easier than a western, like science fiction. Yes! I could write a space story. My hero would be Buck Galaxy, a rugged astronaut with the strength of ten ordinary men.

Whatever I choose to write, my kindest moments picture me laboring away in my own private grotto, ala Dickens, bringing life to some circumstance and breath to a person who, until now, did not exist. And I have wondered — who are they who have lived only within my brain until this moment when, poof! Here they are?

Is there a universe, veiled and mysterious, obscure and secret, that awaits only a key for it to blossom into nova and project its brightness, however momentary, where there was but darkness moments before? Does that universe also comprise myriad stars and comets, planets and seas, continents and cities, houses and grottos where someone else creates something from where there was once, nothing?

Such weighty questions!

Perhaps universes prevail within us all and only a fortunate few are able to find the key. Let's go one step further and consider whether it is likewise possible that such persons and their universe, once given sustenance and being, shall ever perish. It seems quite plausible that literary universes, once born, endure forever. There remains then the problem of not only creating our particular universes but also insuring their continuous life span. That's where editors come in. It is necessary to convince an editor of the value in publishing our little stories, which are the building blocks of literary universes.

Writers have strange ideas why editors reject their perfect manuscripts. Some believe it to be a matter of jealousy. Others think editors fear them. Neither of these contentions has genuine merit. Why is this so? The answer is simple.

You see, there is no such thing as an editor!

An editor is actually a figment of imagination. A fictitious intermediary. A contrivance invented by publishers to avoid condemnation by hopeful authors for having to return unwanted submissions. Yet, despite contrary evidence, there are still many writers who are reluctant to accept this truism. They continue to disregard the unsigned rejection notice that perpetuates this myth through the editorial use of plural personal pronouns.

"**We** are sorry but your manuscript is not quite right for **our** current needs. Thank you for thinking of **us**. [from] OBNOXIOUS PRESS."

Publishers would have us believe they are basically nice folks who unintentionally employed a Scrooge as editor and there is nothing they (the publishers) can do about it. If they (the publishers) were the final authority in the matter, they (the publishers) would publish everything that writers submit. But because of the ogre editor, such cannot be the case.

This type of deceptive practice is not unheard of in the commonplace business world. Movie stars use stand-ins to act for them on occasion. The United States Army has fancifully created Sergeants for dirty work and Presidents have their CIAs. Even Oliver North used a ... he had a ... come to think of it, Ollie was probably the lone exception to this rule.

There must be special courses in publishing school for teaching how to reject manuscripts while presenting the rejection as the unfeeling act of a nonexistent editor. These courses would probably include a section on "Facetious Comments" such as "We think this is your best work thus far — Sorry, but keep trying!" A subcourse would undoubtedly cover "Misplaced SASEs," plus "Appropriated Paper Clips," and "Anthology Sales Pitch 101."

Writers become paranoid after numerous rejections. They then attempt to overcome their failures by trying to please a phantom editor. A poet from Michigan once submitted four short poems, double-spaced, centered on individual pages and each with a tiny chocolate candy kiss affixed to the upper right corner. The poems were subsequently returned with a plural personal pronoun rejection — minus the kisses.

Another unpublished author of confession stories included a photograph with her manuscript showing a rather shapely young lady. She was quite chagrined to receive a rejection signed by three supposed editors, each of whom requested additional photos.

The best way to beat the system is to purchase a printing press or a computer with desktop publishing capability and issue a regular publication. Of course, the writer immediately becomes a publisher himself and must therefore invent an ogre editor so he (the writer/publisher) can freely reject manuscripts by using the professional plural personal pronoun publication procedure.

CHAPTER SIX

An alarming number of poets and writers have admittedly been entertained by strange and eerie voices during particularly vulnerable moments in which they were most receptive to creative ideas. Edgar Allan Poe once confessed that he was often hounded by echoes flitting from side to side in his bedchamber while biding time with impatience, paper and pen for his ever-active brain to select a poetic theme.

Thomas Moore related an overheard conversation that only a poet of his stature would dare acknowledge.

> *The black eye may say, "Come and worship my ray;*
> *By adoring, perhaps you may move me."*
> *But the blue eye, half hid, says, from under its lid,*
> *"I love, and am yours, if you love me!"*

Literary folks are especially susceptible to hearing inner voices simply because they seem to be forever listening for them. They attribute the resultant verses and poetic prose to lyric muses lest they be judged somewhat suspect in the area of mental competence. Noted psychologists refer to this passing of the buck as subtle evidence of schizophrenia, or dual personalities. It's actually a rather common practice among those whose fertile minds experience few limitations in the pursuit of ideas set forth in memorable verse.

John Greenleaf Whittier was supposedly influenced by an

angel whispering to him, "Be resigned: Bear up, bear on, the end shall tell; the dear Lord ordereth all things well." Ralph Waldo Emerson said that the snow arrives announced by all the "trumpets of the sky," and Tennyson interpreted for us the song of a brook as it came from "haunts of coot and hern; as it made a sudden sally, sparkling out among the fern to bicker down a valley."

Emily Dickinson wrote of many conversations with nature and with Death itself while Shakespeare tuned in repeatedly to all of the muses in his dramatic plays and poems of love. Others were inspired by beauty, romance, war, or humor ascribing their creative efforts to personal experience and yet, their phrases hint of spirit voices not of their own consciousness. Even contemporary writers are making known the voices that speak to them of many things. Edgar Bowers acknowledged, "What I might be I learned to tell in eyes which loved me. Voices formed my name."

I, too, have been mindful of whispers from undetermined sources in the wee hours of the night or when nodding surreptitiously during church services on sultry Sunday mornings. It was usually those occasions that gave rise to my most prolific creations. Of course, not a few of these voices may be credited to an unsympathetic spouse who, with repeated jabs of her elbow, advised regarding unwelcome reverberating sounds emitting from my ever active brain which was working hard to select the proper theme for my next creative effort.

I futilely tried explaining how an artist's mind never sleeps.

Other voices have presented themselves at decidedly inconvenient occasions, on the downtown commuter bus for instance amid an assortment of traveling tradespeople and the usual peripheral dopers, truants, and muggers. I recall one episode while catnapping when I accidentally startled a hand searching within my inside coat pocket. My muse was in the process of proposing an ingenious ending for a mystery novel that had been in limbo for weeks.

My eyelids snapped open and I exclaimed aloud, "That's it!"

"What's it, man! I didn't do nothing!" The hand was apparently attached to a pockmarked face, complete with curled black sideburns and thin underdeveloped moustache. The apparition was last seen making hurried tracks to the back of the bus, seeking anonymity. Paying no further attention, I devoted the next several minutes to making rapid notations in my small simulated leather notebook. It was essential that the voice's message be recorded as accurately as possible until I could return home and complete my writing project at leisure.

I will be the first to concede that many of my stories and little verses are suggested by my muse, who is without name but is the possessor of a multitude of identities. She (a little sexism here) is equally proficient at speaking in the voice of Poe or Millay, Frost or Stevenson, Arthur Conan Doyle or either of the Brownings while allowing me to do the actual writing and to receive the byline. It's a perfect arrangement and similar, I suspect, to arrangements she has engineered with other writers and poets in other places and in other times.

It may have been the reason why a friend once asked if I believed in reincarnation. The question stemmed from an observation that my work seemed styled from the past. Therefore, the query, "Are you actually a poet from ages ago?"

It was long in coming but my secret was finally discovered. I was exposed for what I really am — a shadow of antiquity: For in a previous life I was Tennyson who delighted souls with talk of knightly deeds. In his footsteps I walked the gardens and halls of Camelot as in the days that were and I sang sweet and low to winds of the western sea while my pretty one slept.

I was Robert Burns near the gently flowing Afton where the sweetest hours I ever knew were spent among the lasses O. In the guise of Thomas Moore, I recalled by the smoke that so gracefully curled above green elms that a cottage was near and if peace were to be found in the world, a humble heart might hope for it here.

As Shakespeare I wrote of the paradox of Venus that she is love, she loves, and yet is not loved, and of the death of Adonis; with him is Beauty slain for Chaos comes again. I was surely Wordsworth envisioning a phantom of delight, a spirit, yet a woman too! I wandered lonely as a cloud when all at once I saw a crowd, a host of daffodils, and in my past I was Longfellow pausing between dark and daylight in that time known as the children's hour.

As a poetic writer I lived and as such did I die. I was Robert Louis Stevenson who saw the sailor home from the sea and the hunter home from the hill. I was John Greenleaf Whittier writing for all sad words of tongue or pen, the saddest are "it might have been." I was Eva Rose Park who rests in fragrant bowers bordered with flowers and who shall not pass this way again.

Now that the transparency of my verse and prose has been trumpeted to the world, I must confess that although my words were written in this modern time, they are yet wrapped in the ways of the old. The reality of my pseudonymity was not clearly apparent to my editors or peers and it remained for a friend to innocently and facetiously unmask my subterfuge. To that friend I dedicate a final verse and trust it may serve in vindication.

> From somewhere deep inside,
> Often unexpected,
> Someone shuffles me aside,
> Usurping, undetected;
> In my skin and bones he walks
> And with my lips he talks.
> No one knows he isn't me
> None suspects my quandary,
> For with my hand he pens a rhyme
> Patterned from an ancient time
> And all who read such verses written
> Deem me strange, unduly smitten
> With such style from long ago
> Availed by Edgar Allan Poe.
> Boundless wealth of haunting phrases
> By his master hand does fall
> While I accept such welcome praises
> As if I earned them all.

CHAPTER SEVEN

Our language is full of beautiful words. Aspiring writers need look no further than the poesy of Byron.

She walks in beauty, like the night
Of cloudless climes and starry skies,
And all that's best of dark and bright
Meets in her aspect and her eyes.

I suspect, however, the presence of an unwritten law requiring an equal percentage of irritating or peevish words unattractive to the eye and just plain ugly when spoken aloud. Scholars contend that the English language is confusing enough with words spelled differently but having similar meaning and words with similar sounds but dissimilar spelling or definition. Perhaps writers, being attuned to the tonal timbre of words, tend to become aggravated and impatient with certain words of unpoetic patterns.

Consider for example, iterate and reiterate. If a person iterates once, is it then possible to reiterate, or to iterate again? And if someone iterates twice, is there any need to reiterate, ever? Then there are flammable and inflammable. I once observed two fuel trucks on the highway. One had a sign warning that its contents were flammable while the other claimed that its cargo was inflammable. I suppose both were inflammatory but were either of them flammatory?

Let's not even discuss affluence and effluence.

Many words with x's, g's, or k's, are often objectionable in appearance and quality of sound. Personally, I am really not too fond of q's either. There is something harsh and displeasing in most words containing these letters that seem to grate against every nerve fiber in my body. I can be quite absorbed in a clever adventure or mystery story until the hero is described as egregious. That's when I begin to lose interest.

There is nothing remotely poetic about such words as noxious, aghast, mannikin, or ubiquitous. Oh, they're perfectly good words. I don't mean to demean them at all but try fitting them into a sonnet.

Poets who pursued their art during the Ancient and Romantic Ages can possibly be excused for employing abstract words because of the relative limitations of early vocabularies and their desire for innovation. But in this modern era, Walt Whitman and I for instance, despite his lusty leaves of grass, would seldom have seen eye to eye on the poeticism of certain words and phrases. He doted on iterations and non-rhyme and infrequences such as plenteous, outvied, rhythmus, intermits, eclaircise, rondure, et al. I learned to keep a thesaurus handy when reading his immodest articulations.

The repute of a poet has eternally been marked by the range of his language vocabulary and the adeptness by which he manipulates words into memorable phrases. Never has it depended upon an addictive inclination for unsightly or discordant words. Contemporary users of four-letter profanities should take due notice.

Moments of circumstance and fervent emotions present favorable opportunities for composing poetry that may be enhanced by the selection of words that are precisely descriptive. Words carelessly interjected frequently conflict with poetic intention. This is usually the result of writing in haste and is subsequently compounded by an impatience to work on another project. When this happens we simply defend our shortcomings by declaring, "Words fail me."

I suspect it isn't the words that have failed.

It's difficult enough for writers who work at home to arrange words on paper in a manner either pleasing or educational with the expectation of selling them to a publisher. It is even more so when faced with obstacles that must be hurdled or at the least, brushed aside without dropping a comma or quotation mark.

"Be very quiet, children. Don't disturb your father."

"But what's he doing in there, mama?"

"He's writing dear. Now be good children and run along."

"We want to help. Why can't we help, mama?"

"Because he's creating and he has to do that by himself."

"Why, mama?"

Of course, even through the closed bedroom door, our hero cannot help but hear the plaintive cries and questions from those too young to understand that although daddy is at home, he is also working. It would do little good to attach a Do Not Disturb sign on the door. There would only be more questions, in shrill loud little voices, about why the sign is hanging there. Better to stick cotton in the ears and keep plugging away.

The writer at home can work through minor distractions as long as the words continue to flow freely but he begins paying his dues when the dam starts to dry up. Sitting there staring at a blank sheet of paper or computer screen with that incessant blinking cursor soon wears thin. Even the ticking of a clock becomes nerve jangling.

"Stop that racket!" he mutters under his breath. But the clock keeps ticking and the cursor continues to blink accusingly. From somewhere, the buzzing of a fly becomes louder with each passing minute. "How can anyone concentrate with all this noise?" His eye catches the flight path of the offending insect as it defiantly swoops past him out of reach. Rising slowly from his chair, our writer hero stealthily takes hold of last month's issue of Modern Poetry and rolls it up tightly into a fearful weapon while he stalks the fly in its journey around the room. Once it darts near enough to coax a wild swing but escapes unscathed and lands on the lampshade to cling and snicker in taunting glee.

Now our writer calls upon his experience in stalking pesky flies. He recalls that common knowledge has dictated how most flies will rise upward and slightly backward, a fact that has been filed away for just such a moment.

So far, so good. The fly is still cleaving to the lampshade. Our hero tightens his grip on the rolled-up magazine and draws back his arm for a swing. Aiming slightly behind his target, he brings the weapon down swiftly and unerringly as the prey begins its takeoff. However, despite established theory, this time the fly's flight pattern is straight up and forward and it is the lamp that falls victim to the attack. With a loud crash it bounces off the wall and hits the floor, separating bulb and shade upon impact.

"Are you all right, dear?"

"I'm fine. Everything's OK."

"Is daddy still creating, mama?"

"Hush children. Yes, your father is still creating."

"He sure creates loud, don't he, mama?"

CHAPTER EIGHT

Imagination allowed me to talk with Edgar Allan Poe in a posthumous interview. Widely acclaimed as the originator of the detective story and stylist of the macabre, Poe died under mysterious circumstances on October 7, 1849 and was buried in Westminster churchyard in Baltimore. The interview proceeded as follows.

Now, Mister Poe, for the benefit of our readers and to set the record straight, let me point out that you requested this interview.

"Yes, that is correct."

May I ask the reason for this extraordinary event?

"Well sir, as you undoubtedly are aware, I have suffered enormous adverse media coverage following my untimely demise back in forty-nine."

They say you were zonked out on drugs.

"That's exactly what I'm talking about! I never used the stuff. Oh, I tippled occasionally — perhaps a glass of sherry to be sociable."

As I understand it, you downed more than your share of the grape and even lost a job or two because of your fondness for strong drink.

"Jealousy, sheer jealousy. There were some publishers who resented the tremendous success of my tales of supernatural horror and accused me of poisoning the minds of young readers. According to them my stories were neurotic and bordering the rim of insanity. They called me crazy Eddie!"

Is that when you turned to drugs?

"Young man, you're beginning to try my patience. I do hereby officially and for all time deny that I ever popped a pill, sniffed a snort or shot a vein. I don't pretend that such things were unheard of in my time. On the contrary, I had an acquaintance or two in the army who were known to puff on a taro root from time to time but I resisted the temptation. Such things were unbecoming of a career military man. Did you know that I held the rank of Sergeant Major and that I later attended West Point?"

I heard you were expelled. Was it your drinking?

"Absolutely not! Wine was not permitted at the academy. No, I couldn't abide all those stupid drills. We were forced to march up and down all the time. Hup! Hoop! Twip! Fwup! Not only that but everything had to be spick and span and polished and trimmed and neat. It was all nonsense. I flunked out on purpose."

I see.

"Don't get me wrong, boy! I loved military life. I even served another hitch after that but that's another story."

OK. Let's move on to what happened in Baltimore.

"First, you have to realize that it was a very traumatic time for me. My wife was only two years in her grave. I drank to forget and when that failed, I drank some more. I tried courting other ladies and even wrote poems to win their favor. Are you familiar with, 'Helen, thy beauty is to me like those Nicean barks of yore, that gentle, after a perfumed sea, the weary, way-worn wanderer bore to him his own native shore?' "

Yes, I am. I am especially fond of the second verse. "On desperate seas long wont to roam, thy hyacinth hair, thy classic face, thy Naiad airs have brought me home to the glory that was Greece and the grandeur that was Rome."

"It's a lousy poem. Take my word for it. I stole it."

You stole it?

"Sure, I read somewhere about Grecian glory and Roman grandeur, so I borrowed it. It's no big deal."

What! Edgar Allan Poe steals a poem and it's not a big deal?

"Happens all the time."

I can't believe it.

"I also wrote pilfered poems to Annie, Lenore, Eulalie and a few others who shall remain nameless. They're all lousy poems."

What about . . . Annabel Lee?

"Ah yes, Annabel Lee. A lovely lady but we're straying from the subject at hand."

Baltimore?

"Baltimore."

Tell me about Baltimore.

"It was unseasonably cold. Snow was on the ground and I just arrived to keep a lecture appointment. The Raven was still enjoying a popular reception around the country and that ominous black bird was proving to be a rich financial resource. The Baltimore Literary Society invited me to discuss the poem at their state convention. It was at the train station that I encountered a somewhat attractive young lady and we agreed to enjoy each other's company at a nearby inn. Her name was Sarah and she proved to be not unfamiliar with that area of the city. She gently guided me as we trudged arm-in-arm along darkened streets through the falling snow."

Do you mean to say you were picked up by a hooker?

"Don't interrupt."

Sorry.

"Anyway, there I was, in a strange town with a lonely night ahead of me. What was wrong with a little friendly companionship? It was very cold. Did I mention that? Anyway, we walked on and the wintry wind blew with a fury I had not previously imagined. The driving snow blinded me to our surroundings until at last I sighted a dim street light and I surmised we had reached our intended destination. We paused momentarily and Sarah turned to me with a smile and outstretched arms. Perhaps it was a bit kinky but I opened my coat to better experience the warmth of her eager body as my arms sought to enfold her. Our lips pressed and the mounting storm subsided with the ecstasy of our kiss.

"Suddenly I felt the sharp bite of an assassin's knife. Blood gushed forth from the wound that rent the vessels of my heart. It was Sarah who held the blade and who now watched as my life drained upon the snow at her feet.

"In anger she did wield the knife. Her passion forfeited my life while formless vapors gathered 'round to cloak her victim on the ground. Although I lay apart from she, her mind was yet aware of me for as my final breath drew nearer she brought forth a pocket mirror. Before my eyes it grew and glowed expanding as a magic flowed. It was through that gateway Sarah strode and vanished into the mirror!"

Are you trying to tell me that this chick stabbed you and then made a getaway by stepping into a magic mirror?

"That's exactly what happened."

But none of the newspapers reported that you were found in a pool of blood.

"It was hushed up."

Why? Who?

"I can only say that Sarah was the Devil's pawn."

What do you mean?

"I'm sorry but my time has expired."

Wait a minute! You can't leave it like that.

"The full story has been related in a manuscript which I was later able to ghost write."

A manuscript? Where is it? Who has it?

"There is nothing else to say except that your quest may be likened to that of the gallant knight who, gaily bedight in sunshine and in shadow, journeyed long, singing a song, in search of El Dorado."

By virtue of this interview with Poe I felt a special dispensation to parody his poem of The Raven.

Once upon a midnight dreary while reviewing a tale by Poe, I heard a curious rapping, a gentle tapping at my cottage door.

"How very strange," I muttered as I rose from my chair and opened the door to find nobody there! It was a wintry evening and the crackling hearth doubtless confused my ears as did its misshapen shadows befuddle my eyes. "Pure imagination," I chuckled aloud. "And wouldn't Edgar himself be proud?" Again came the rapping from my cottage door but I knew it was illusion. Only that and nothing more.

Back inside, the fire burned brightly as a chill crept ever slightly from my head down to my toes. Perhaps the wind blows gustily and bends the supple tree limb thusly to lightly tap upon my door. Surely that and nothing more.

Then at once through the transom flew a stately handsome raven and he perched securely high above my bedroom door. Had I not just read the telling of that ancient bird and the stern decorum of the countenance it wore, I would indeed have been frightened by the manner of its coming and the message I was certain that it bore. But I rather deemed it fortunate for the chance that fate afforded to recount Poe's conversation from the raven's point of view. So it was that I inquired of such incident transpired and I asked this ebon fowl to discourse upon its famed debut.

But not a word escaped the ominous bird from its perch above the door and I began to doubt such words that I had read before. "Tell me, Raven," said I. "Truly are you he who left a token of despair by one word spoken in response to earnest pleadings for the maiden named Lenore?"

Still no sound forthcoming from the raven and I pondered once again of its purpose as it perched atop my bedroom door. So I mused that by tomorrow it would leave, yet somewhere I recalled such musing made before.

"You remind me of a story," I directed this at him. "A tale once told in drawing rooms of a raven ghastly grim who wandered far from Pluto's shore and settled for the night above a friendly chamber door. Such a bird it was that sat upon a sculptured Pallas and foretold of dire things while not departing from its demon throne. It is said that the raven, never flitting, still is sitting while the lamplight throws its shadow on the floor."

Not once by even a simple nodding did the bird acknowledge my prodding so I vowed to press it even that much more. "With due respect," I said, "I fondly hope that you are prepared to cope with a stay as lengthy as forevermore for you see, I lately applied your perching spot with the contents of an old glue pot and so I fear your searching for a home may be ever o'er."

With that, the raven made a lurch and flew at once from off its perch above my bedroom door. I flung open the shutter and with scarcely a flutter my unwelcome guest through the window did soar. "Lies! Lies!" it shrieked as into the night it streaked before circling back once more. Declaimed the raven, "There is no worse crime than incessant rhyme from punsters who are genuinely a bore and for the sake of a tale that epigrammatists regale, my role has been an insufferable chore. I'll not, therefore, dwell again among callous mortal men.

"No!" said the raven.

"Nevermore!"

CHAPTER NINE

Moving to a new town can be frightening, especially if the wife has a full-time job and the man of the house is a writer.

"Oh look, Henry! There goes the missus off to work while he stays at home and probably sleeps until noon or watches soap operas on the television."

"Hush Ethel. It's none of our business if the mister wants to be a house-husband."

"He says he's a writer but I think it's just an alibi because he can't earn an honest living.

"Don't be too harsh on him, dear. I'm sure he's nice to his mother."

It makes no difference how much effort the writer makes to be charming. Friendly waves and lots of smiles. People are naturally suspicious of any man who doesn't leave the house for eight hours of work each day. Perhaps they suspect him of being on the FBI most wanted list and he's merely hiding out until the heat dies down. They probably expect to see the SWAT team surrounding the house at any moment.

At first the neighbors may have thought he worked for a newspaper or magazine publisher and mused how nice it would be to have a celebrity living in their midst. Who could blame them for not knowing that freelance writers have no office to go to except for the spare upstairs bedroom? Some may be more curious than others at what goes on in the house while the wife is away. Once or twice they even telephone to ask if he would mind driving them to the grocery or drug store on the pretext that their car won't start.

"I hate to bother you, Tom," they say. "But I knew you were home and not doing anything important."

Maybe they think he is spying on them to obtain material for a gossip column or a smutty novel. I'm sure he often feels like dropping a veiled hint about one of his story characters leaving their husband to elope with the Orkin man, just to observe any reaction. The wife has already warned him about his overactive imagination and not to allow little things to bother him. She assures him that Mrs. Baker across the street didn't really mean to imply that he was operating a shady mail order business or even authoring illegal chain letters.

A most annoying habit of new neighbors is to drop over for a visit to interrogate the writer about his writing. "Would I recognize anything you have written?"

He would love to answer, "Hah! You can't even recognize your own front door at two in the morning."

"How much money do you make with your little stories?"

With a searing stare, his wife cuts off his intended reply.

"Have you ever thought about getting a real job?"

Under his breath comes a mumble, "Have you ever thought of being knocked through my picture window?"

It may take a few weeks but everyone soon learns to talk to him only in his wife's presence. She readily explains to them what he meant to say and to please ignore his artistic temperament. Eventually the day arrives when peace descends upon the writer's private little corner of the world and he can stop worrying about getting his house rolled in bathroom tissue. Of course, that signals a time to move on and break in a new neighborhood.

Whatever success I have enjoyed as a writer is definitely unrelated to any tendency I may have for maintaining a detached attitude during stressful situations. Sunday was a good example.

While I struggled to put the finishing touches on a travel article, I was suddenly shaken by loud rolling peals of thunder and a jagged flash of lightning. I was already into an extended deadline and the final segment was proceeding smoothly from my old Underwood when the desk lamp faltered. Annoyed at the interruption I groped through the darkness and located the wall switch after tripping over the dog. However, no amount of flipping, cursing, or yapping would turn the lights back on.

My article had to be mailed the next morning so there was nothing to do but complete it by flashlight — if only I could remember where I put it. I may have used it to flush out a cat from underneath my GMC pickup. With that possibility in mind I gingerly made my way through the darkened house and emerged into the garage. The dog, having already been stepped on once, remained at my heel until I opened the truck door. He immediately bounded past me with a blur onto the front seat to await his customary ride. I opened the glove box and there was the flashlight, but the switch failed to produce the expected ray of light.

The batteries were dead.

I began to panic. Rivulets of perspiration trickled down my side. For an eternity I felt the pounding of my heart while my brain labored to resolve my plight.

Candles! That was the answer.

A vague remembrance hinted of a birthday party two years ago. Again I returned to the house and rummaged through kitchen cabinets before locating a small box containing five thin candles. "Enough," I thought, "to survive through the remaining three or four pages of my draft."

At my desk I positioned the lighted candles for maximum visibility. I faced the typewriter and reviewed my last paragraph but the words were not clear in the flickering light. I would have to work fast and so began punching keys with determination.

The candlelight was waning noticeably and my right index finger promptly missed the j and lodged between the k and l. I was unable to locate the -, the ", or the (), and my nose nearly rested on the space bar in a frantic search for the?. I anticipated much greater difficulty in finding the . and the '. I usually experienced enough trouble in the light of day converting . and ' into ! so this time I would forego it for the remainder of my article.

I remarked to myself how fortunate not to be creating a poem because every poet knows how nearly impossible it is to create verse without using one or more !'s.

Seldom do we notice the relative importance of those other infrequently used symbols on the typewriter and on computer keyboards? You know, the @, the &, the +, the ¶, the #, the [] and the *. Oh sure, we're more familiar with the regular letter keys. Still, the @, &, +, ¶, #, [], and the * are there for a reason and it would be reprehensible, perhaps even sinful, not to make use of them if only occasionally to make sure they are still in good working order.

Some folks might believe these particular keys to be practically useless and that they were placed on keyboards primarily as a decorative scheme to enhance the elegance of a new product.

"Honey, look at the cute little wiggles on these keys."

"They're not wiggles, Gladys. They perform certain functions."

"Oh, I know dear but aren't they cute? Especially the little tic-tac-toe."

"Gladys, don't you know anything? That's the sign for pounds or to show a number."

"Really! Well how about the little star?"

"The little star is called an asterisk and it's used as a footnote."

"Gee you're smart, Harry."

"Well, I didn't go to college but I do know a few things."

Proofreaders have found these little wiggles invaluable in alerting typesetters where paragraphs should begin or where to insert explanatory words and phrases. Some of the symbols are used in marketing to denote individual unit costs while others are useful in mathematical functions or to identify mergers.

In spite of our taking them for granted because of their intermittent and casual appearances in areas neither journalistic nor literary, the @, &, +, ¶, #, [], and * each brings a classic atmosphere of style and tone whenever they are dutifully called upon.

Besides, most of us have to agree . . . they are kinda cute!

CHAPTER TEN

Writers are not poets just because they can string two rhyming couplets together, nor because of the awards adorning their wall. Not until they successfully pass the poet's quiz. So sharpen your wits out there, square your roundels, concentrate and see how many of the following poetic terms you are able to correctly define.

1. Haiku:
a) An uncontrollable sneeze
b) A Japanese automobile.
c) Baby's first word

2. Edgar Allan Poe:
a) The founder of Poe Folks Restaurant
b) An alias used by John Dillinger
c) The Ames Brothers

3. Dimeter:
a) A meter that's hard to see
b) Distance from one side of a circle to the other
c) A bad word uttered in frustration

4. Wordsworth:
a) How payment is determined for a poetic essay
b) Second cousin of Henry Wadsworth Longfellow
c) Less value than pagesworth

5. Sicilian Octave:
a) They're black and served on a relish tray
b) A mafia assassin
c) One range lower than a French octave

6. Rhythm:
a) A one and a two and a three
b) You either got it or you don't got it
c) A method of birth control

7. Alliteration:
a) An uneducated poet
b) Erased completely
c) Born of unwed parents

8. Allegory:
a) They have big teeth and live in Florida
b) A scary story with lots of blood and icky stuff
c) Something that makes you sneeze

9. Epigrams:
a) A lengthy message sent by Western Union
b) Letters worn on a favorite sweater
c) A contagious disease

10. Irony:
a) Housewives must finish this before writing poetry
b) Heavy metal rock groups on MTV
c) Natives of Iran

Scoring: Ten right —You're not to be trusted at all
Five right —You don't fully understand what's happening
Three right —You've taken this test before
Two right —There's hope for you yet
One right   —You passed with honors

True poets know it's a fact how readers will pass up a poem

that appears at first glance to be long-winded and monotonous. It may be a classic of the lyric art but its visual appearance can project it as unexciting and rather boring. What is the secret then that magically entices a reader to pause long enough to read the opening lines of a poem?

The answer is white space.

White space is that portion of the page on which there are no words or lines to clutter up the visual pattern of a poem. It is the hook that grabs a browser as he is about to turn the page. An average reader will instinctively shudder when first encountering long sentences from margin to margin, especially when they form paragraphs of formidable size. The preference is for short lines and brief stanzas. This is best accomplished by the use of white space.

It's a ploy long practiced by novelists to break up the monotony of block paragraphs and also serves as a resting place for weary eyes. Writers use white space liberally by a deliberate shortening of sentences. This results in several lines consisting of one or two words giving the appearance that the rest of the page is uncluttered. Many writers accomplish a preponderance of white space by inserting dialogue at strategic intervals.

"How," you may ask, "does this work?"

"Simple. We are employing it now."

"You mean, that's all there is to it?"

"Exactly."

The white space thus generated implies that the story is an exciting one. The reader's interest is thus captured. He continues to read if only to satisfy his curiosity and if the writer has any talent at all, the unfolding tale will keep the reader absorbed. Naturally, a mediocre story defeats the reader's patience and he moves on.

It's the same with a poem.

Poetry is more complex than prose. Poets must deal with creating an impact with as few words as possible while a novelist can fill page after page with trivialities until an eventual climax is reached. For this reason, white space becomes crucial to the success of a poem.

Consider Shelley. A supreme poet of the same stature as Byron and Tennyson, he is nonetheless often tedious with his interminable lack of white space. It is only his tercets that preserve his honored status because they present an attractive page of easy reading. His "Ode To The West Wind" is a prime example.

> "O wild West Wind, thou breath of Autumn's being
> Thou, from whose unseen presence the leaves dead
> Are driven, like ghosts from an enchanter fleeing.
>
> "Yellow, and black, and pale, and hectic red,
> Pestilence-stricken multitudes: O thou,
> Who chariotess to their dark wintry bed
>
> "Thy wingéd seeds, where they lie cold and low,
> Each like a corpse within its grave, until
> Thine azure sister of the Spring shall blow . . ."

Notice how the white space sets off the lines and lures the reader into what may otherwise appear to be a ponderous poem and yet turns out to be quite enjoyable. That is the mark of a master poet. This is not to imply that a poet can write any old thing, embellish it with garlands of white space, and see it accepted as quality poetry. Just as in a novel, a poem must be good to start with to hold a reader's attention. But it is white space that can give it a chance to be read by momentarily halting an impatient eye and allowing the poem to work whatever magic it possesses.

Sometimes the best part of a poem is the nothingness surrounding it.

Romantic prose has been known to spice up a poet's literary creations with words not ordinarily used in everyday conversation. It has ever been so.

Recognizing that a vast misunderstanding has existed for centuries in interpretations of the works proffered by past masters of the poetic arts, I have undertaken an encyclopedic study of the problem. My purpose is purely academic and intended solely as a service to readers and beginning poets alike. So without further ado, I hereby present a brief synopsis of my thesaurus.

O'er—Shakespeare used it to save writing space and was seldom up a creek without one
Ponder—Poets do this when their rent is overdue
Gambol—To cavort about in delightful innocent play. (Not to be confused with the Las Vegas variety)
Alas—A young unmarried girl in Scotland
Alack—A lad without alas
Climes—They were first grown in the Garden of Eden
Dactyl—A big prehistoric bird
Prithee—Another of Shakespeare's favorite words. It is today that little building in the farmer's back yard
Midst—A low cloud that hovers over swamps and haunted houses
Soliloquy—A speech that no one is supposed to hear
Hail—An exclamation of disbelief; i.e., "The hail you say!"
Afar—Something to keep you warm on a cold winter night
Whither—Where
Hither—Here
Thither—A musical instrument
Tryst—A dance invented by Chubby Checker
Bard—Someone who has just met an angry bear
Ultimus— Final entry, or the end, which this is.

CHAPTER ELEVEN

If I have any advice at all for people with stars in their eyes who aspire to become successful writers, it can be summed up in one word — perseverance. That is what spells the difference between Stephen King and Oscar Liverwitz, You may rightfully ask who is Oscar Liverwitz to which I can reply, "No one knows."

See what I mean?

Perhaps if Oscar Liverwitz had not given up after his manuscript was rejected for the tenth time his name might be a household word today in book stores around the world.

Suppose the Wright Brothers had crawled out of the wreckage of their first flying machine to exclaim, "Whew! Never again!" What if the creator of Superman stopped short with, "Look! Up in the Sky! It's . . . oh, uh, never mind. It's only a bird." What if Poe had shredded The Raven manuscript because he couldn't get it past the transom reader? Furthermore, at this point I would be remiss if I failed to mention that only by perseverance did two snails reach Noah's ark prior to the great storm.

They're all now enshrined in the HOFP — the Hall Of Fame for Perseverers. Every wannabe writer has to ask himself if he is ready and willing to sacrifice hours of sleep whenever an idea strikes him because he must then trundle out of bed to record the passing thought before it fades into oblivion. Is he able to withstand the constant rejection by editors and the criticism of his peers just for a byline? Can he continue churning out those poems, essays and short stories one by one despite the possibility that no one may ever read them? Is he independently wealthy or at least the incumbent of a steady job? If these questions can be answered affirmatively, without hedging, there is a chance our wishful prosaist may one day find himself listed on the pages of Redbook or perhaps on the shelves at B. Dalton.

But it takes perseverance.

First of all, writing must be regarded as a business. It should be looked upon as the product of a manufacturing firm; to be designed, assembled, tested, polished, marketed, and if necessary, to be remodeled and remarketed. The research department concentrates on determining where there is a market for the writing product while the quality control staff ensures that the product has attained the desired level of competitive value. The sales force keeps knocking on editorial doors and the shipping clerks package the product attractively and mail it timely to meet schedules or deadlines. A breakdown of one of these departments results in a profit loss for the entire firm.

Each writer then is President, Executive Manager, and Foreman. It is his responsibility to make his business produce and prosper and he can best accomplish this through perseverance.

This insistent quality can also be utilized to overcome certain poetic products that may be difficult to market. For instance, poetic masters are lauded for their artistic attainment, and rightfully so. It is irrelevant that many of their literary creations are simply misunderstood by the common man. Let me prove my point.

T.S. Eliot, one of the most influential poets of our time, was educated at Harvard, the Sorbonne, and at Oxford, and in 1948 he won the Nobel Prize for Literature. One of his most notable poems was The Hollow Man with its familiar ending, "This is the way the world ends/Not with a bang but a whimper." Within that same poem there is another less memorable stanza.

> "Here we go round the prickly pear
> Prickly pear prickly pear
> Here we go round the prickly pear
> At five o'clock in the morning."

Now I ask you, does that sound like the work of a master poet? It may be argued that Prickly Pear is an unfair example. Perhaps T.S. was feeling poorly that day. Nay, I say NAY, for he is further credited with the following muddled statement. "I take as metaphysical poetry that in which what is ordinarily apprehensible only by thought is brought within the grasp of feeling, or that in which what is ordinarily only felt is transformed into thought without ceasing to be feeling."

Being the common man that I am, I can only ask, "Huh?"

Equally profound musings were uttered by that patriarch of free verse, Mr. Walt Whitman. In Leaves Of Grass he wrote, "I do not snivel that snivel the world over, that months are vacuums and the ground but wallow and filth. Whimpering and truckling fold with powders for invalids, conformity goes to the fourth-remov'd." Undoubtedly believing he had us on the ropes at this juncture, he then delivered an off-hand reference to "scented herbage of my breast." Whatever his intended message; being a common man, I suggest that old Walt waxed overly poetic with that one.

Rudyard Kipling once spoke of "the heave and the halt and the hurl and the crash of the comber wind-hounded," while Emily Bronte gave us "the plashing of the surge." Not to be undone, John Clare presented little Trotty Wagtail who "waddled in the water-pudge and waggle went his tail."

Shakespearean devotés may be acquainted with, "It was a lover and his lass, with a hey, and a ho, and a hey nonino," from As You Like It. But if this seemingly fails to measure up to the Bard's usual level of genius, consider the following verse.

> "Where the bee sucks, there suck I,
> In a cowslip's bell I lie,
> There I couch when owls do cry,
> On the bat's back I do fly."

It is doubtful that the American Poetry Review would express serious interest in any of the above passages if received one morning over the transom. Furthermore, in his soliloquy of

Hamlet to the fair Ophelia, Mr. Shakespeare confusingly declaimed "to be or not to be" as being the question but he then completely failed to provide the answer.

Contemporary poets have similarly contributed to the obscurities of modern poetry. Let us examine a few choice phrases beginning anonymously with; "Like a flickering ember, we are engulfed in the mood of the times and it is thus easier to accede, thereby to prosper without endeavor than to nurture a kindled spark and reap an eventual flame." Citing another illustration we have, "You and I, we are all that we are and all that we hope to be. Yet, in each of us lies that which yearns for what we wished to be."

It is certain that these great compositions are quite pithy in their meaningful content but a common man like myself finds them somewhat of an impediment in my continued search for good poetry.

> Oh, would that I were cleverish
> To justify a gifting wish.

CHAPTER TWELVE

Humor is a subject in which everyone is an expert although some may be more expert than others. For the serious student of humor, it can actually be divided into two departments. Guffaws form the nucleus of one group while the other comprises tee-hees, snickers, chuckles, giggles, smirks, grins, and otherwise innocuous titters. Webster defines humor as that quality of speech, writing, or action that makes something seem amusing or ludicrous. It is a unique quality found only in humans and some primates but certainly not in other animals in spite of imprecise references to horse laughs, hen cackles, or even a laughing stock.

Humorists come in three sizes. One employs irony and satire to point out the absurd while another prefers lyricism to provide a gentle or wry interpretation. Last but not least is the specie that delights in using a pun or two just for the hell of it. The degree of amusement in any situation is largely dependent upon the relative viewpoints of both the humorist and the humoree, keeping in mind that it is often funnier to wield the weapon of wit than to feel its barb.

The value of humor was recognized by Will Rogers who once remarked, "We are all here for a spell, so get all the good laughs you can." He also proposed that the most prolific inspirations for humor were government, taxes, and sex — not necessarily in that order.

Not many people are aware that in the 16th century, the word "humour" denoted an unbalanced mental condition, which some may insist yet prevails in some semblance in our modern world. They suggest that for proof one need investigate no further than the sick humor of today's comedic performers. Wit progressed as a form of intellectual quickness, raillery, and repartee, initially dangerous because of its tendency to ridicule religion and moral decency. An inferior literary form, it resulted from a perceived absence of passion and was further caused by certain authors who overly displayed their witticism by attributing them to inappropriate characters.

Satirists abounded during this period. One of their most notable forms of literary humor was that five-line limerick verse, the origin of which is lost in obscurity. It is a kind of ribald epigram disseminated by word of mouth and more often whispered than spoken aloud.

The history of humorous writing has necessarily included sympathy and pathos with lunacy and buffoonery until human nature itself was subtly altered toward sensitivity and a melancholic relief from the sadness of life. Whimsy and mirth soon followed until humor is now identified as the most rounded of all emotions. It is accepted and judged on its merits as would a fine vintage wine or great poetry.

According to Robert Benchley, "Defining and analyzing humor is a pastime of humorless people." Another equally great man commented that nobody truly knows what humor is. People only recognize it when it makes them laugh.

Humor is an extension of the passageways, compartments, and storage chambers of a writer's brain that sustains and nurtures numerous strange thoughts and notions that cause one to question — what if?

For instance, what if Plato had access to a word processor? Well, maybe that's looking too far back in time. All right, what if computers had been available to more contemporary writers such as Shakespeare, Poe or perhaps someone less gifted in literary talent? How about, for the sake of argument, the Lone Ranger?

Imagine how the flavor of the old west was most frequently captured in the waning rays of the setting sun, the lengthening shadows of mesquite, and the rolling tumbleweed. It was the aroma of coffee and the picture of two men huddled over the faint vestige of warmth from a dwindling campfire. One of them wore a white hat and a mask covering his eyes. A six-gun rested on each hip, carried low and tied with a thin leather thong around his leg. It was the mark of a gunfighter.

His faithful companion was an Indian.

Closer scrutiny revealed the masked man painstakingly writing in a small leather-bound book guided only by the light of the flickering campfire as the words emerged on each page. It was his nightly practice to record the events of their daily adventures for posterity, for future generations of mankind, and also for the few bucks earned from the publisher of True Western Tales. Theirs was a life of austerity. Aside from an almost worthless silver mine purchased from a traveling New York peddler, their only income resulted from the sale of dime novels, which barely produced enough funds to keep them in jerky beef and oats for their sturdy mounts.

It was the masked man who wore the white hat, rode the white horse, and jotted down their heroic escapades. But it was the red man's sharp eye and meticulous flair for detail and style that produced the marketable manuscripts that enhanced their status as legends of the old west.

The first draft was routinely submitted for the Indian's editorial review while the author cradled a coffee cup in his hands and waited anxiously for approval. Disappointment often clouded the visible portion of his face upon hearing an unfavorable comment.

"Hunnnh! That not good, Kemosabe."

"What do you mean, not good? What's wrong with it?"

"Bad man, not bad enough," was the brunt reply. "Good man, too good. Pretty girl not smother you with kisses as told on page nine. That part, cut out."

"Cut out? You can't cut that part out. It's romantic. It spices up the story and our stories haven't been too spicy lately."

"Spice not nice, Kemosabe. Hero no need spice. Hero need action. Ride fast horse. Shoot gun. Save ranch. No time waste on spice."

History tells us that the Indian had his way. There was never spice for the masked man as loyal readers later learned in reliving those thrilling days of yesteryear, the cloud of dust, the thundering hooves of that great white horse, and the hearty "Hi Yo, Silver!"

Now, there's a lesson to be learned here.

Perhaps it is the realization that writers and editors are part of a team, with a single purpose. Two heads are better than one, so to speak. Or maybe it's just that the masked man might have been better off with a portable self-contained lap-top PC with a high resolution monitor, 8mb RAM, 1 gigabyte hard drive, a 75,000 word Thesaurus, and user-friendly software. Then again, we may have overlooked the changing of the times and that old ways are sometimes the best ways after all. Perhaps in this modern sophisticated world of literary heroes, spice *is* nice.

Get 'em up Scout!

CHAPTER THIRTEEN

There is a fundamental statute that prescribes how humorists must refrain from attempts to be amusing at home or in front of the neighbors.

"Hey, Tom. I want you to meet my Aunt Ethel. She came all the way from Boise, Idaho. I promised you would say something funny for her. Say something funny, Tom."

Newspaper or magazine columnists are similarly governed by that same law which prohibits them from being humorous for five days out of each week. Three days tops and then only if limited to 500 words per column.

A friend of mine enjoys a favorable reputation for his wit and humorous vignettes. His syndicated work appears on Mondays, Wednesdays and Fridays from Manhattan to Frisco Bay and he drives a BMW during the week, switching to a Jaguar for the weekend. Little does his faithful public realize, however, that every one of his essays are written in less than 500 words. Within that strict limitation my friend is a whimsical pundit, a hilarious satirist, and an all-around entertaining guy. He never submits a column in excess of 500 words because should he proceed, his quips and jests would deflate into unrecognizable blobs. Fame would desert him and GMAC would repossess his BMW.

It seems that a writer's daily creative energy may be fully expended after 500 words and everything goes downhill from there. As is the case with most writers, my friend has discovered that with the 501st word, he turns into a boring, disorganized, rambling unfunny caricature of H. Allen Smith.

Being the frugal persons they are though, most writers do not destroy such pompous prosaic ponderings created during instances in which they do happen to exceed the norm. Instead, they publish them as angry diatribes in volatile attacks against "The System." The system being that nonentity responsible for personal injustices, universal famine, and world wars whenever the exact causes cannot be specifically pinpointed.

All such meanderings possess a melting point at which they succumb to the rigors and pressures of their profession. Their brain waves begin to lose focus and eventually dissipate into scatterings of itinerant rhymes and greeting-card verse. They resort to their poetic beginnings. Strangely enough, their melting point is also 500 words.

As it happens I, too, have felt the urge to be a syndicated columnist and to see my byline appear from coast to coast. I would prefer to write only three days per week and then only 500 words per column. That's in accordance with the unwritten law. However, if a publisher offered me more than a reasonable sum to write a five-day column or a feature with more than 500 words, I would probably agree as long as he realized the probable consequences and was willing to assume the risk. I can certainly be amusing and humorous as well as the next writer in 500 words but then . . . uh, umm, umm.

What was I saying?

It's unfortunate but writers, by the very nature of their profession, have to attend an inordinate number of meetings, conferences and workshops just to rub elbows with other writers, agents, and prospective publishers. It's a way of making contacts and hobnobbing with one's peers. Writer's club meetings are something else. They seem to flourish in every nook and cranny. Some provide an excuse for social gatherings while others apparently exist for the sole purpose of dissecting and tearing apart fellow club members' most recent efforts in the guise of constructing criticism. What follows is a fanciful experience for which some of us can relate.

Once upon a time there was a young poet who labored for many hours until he wrote a beautiful poem. He read it at his poetry club meeting and was critiqued regarding its literary merit.

"It's too long," said club president Mrs. Crabapple.

"Excessively lengthy," agreed school teacher Mary Purkle.

"Far too many words," exclaimed banker Jerome Jones.

"It needs to be shortened," said club critic Alice McCorkle and so the club seemed to speak in one voice.

"All right", said the poet. So he labored far into the night until the poem was half its former size. At the next meeting he read his revised poem and asked for comments.

"It's too short," said Mrs. Crabapple.

"Yes. Exceedingly short," agreed Mary Purkle.

"Not enough words," exclaimed Jerome Jones.

"It should be longer," said Alice McCorkle.

"All right", said the poet and he again labored for many hours until his poem was just the right size. Once more he read it at the club meeting.

"It's too old-fashioned," said Mrs. Crabapple.

"Inconsistent rhyming patterns," said Mary Purkle.

"Too much punctuation," exclaimed Jerome Jones.

"I don't like the title," complained Alice McCorkle.

"Well," said the poet. "I just don't know what else to do with it." So he changed it back to its original form and mailed it to a magazine. In a few weeks he received a letter from the editor. Inside was a check and a notice advising that his beautiful poem would be published in the next issue. The poet announced the news at the next club meeting.

"I am so happy to have helped," said Mrs. Crabapple.

"My suggestions made it so much better," said Mary Purkle.

"You couldn't have done it without me," exclaimed Jerome Jones.

"My contribution is quite evident," crowed Alice McCorkle.

The poet shook his head in disbelief and never said a word to contradict his fellow club members because he did not wish to hurt their feelings. However, from that moment on he wrote his poems and mailed them without consulting anyone as to their literary merit.

And the moral of this story?

*Never trust another
For advice about a poem.
Remember, even Caesar was lost
When all roads led to Roem.*

I have never participated in a professional writing conference or University seminar of the arts but I must admit to a certain degree of curiosity and timid desire to do just that. So after casually broaching the possibility to my wife one evening, I learned that she was not particularly excited over the prospect of my attending such a symposium alone. I have since attempted to recapture a few highlights of our marital discussion on the subject in the following fictionalized vignette.

Newspaper Heading: **SECOND ANNUAL SOUTH-EASTERN WRITERS CONFERENCE IS A SUCCESS.**

"Hello."
"Hello, is this George Phillips?"
"Yes, who is . . . Emily, is that you?"
"It's me, George. I was just wondering how you were getting along at that conference."
"Oh, fine. I'm doing fine, Emily. I just attended a reading by Anthony Winslow VanLandingham III from his best seller 'Nocturnal Nuances'."
"Oh, George. I knew that would happen."
"You knew what would happen?"
"I just knew you would fall in with the wrong crowd."
"What are you talking about, Emily?"
"You know perfectly well, George. That Anthony Whatsisname is the one who writes those horrible limericks I am always finding in your underwear drawer."
"No, no, you're wrong. Wilson Anthony writes those limericks. VanLandingham is an English professor from Fairleigh Dickinson University in New Jersey."

"Just the same, I hope you're not listening to a lot of smut at that get-together of yours."

"Of course not, Emily. I wish you would come with me sometime and see what really happens at these sessions."

"No, thank you. I still remember the last one you went to in Ocala."

"Now, Emily, that wasn't my fault. How was I to know that Xaviera Hollander had been elected poet of the month by the Florida Poetry Society? Besides, the police released us all the very next day."

"All I know is, four girls from my flower club saw that newspaper photo in the Gazette. I still may have to resign from the club."

"Don't worry, Emily. I swear to you that everyone here is only interested in improving their poetry skills and other writing techniques."

"You listen to me, George Phillips. I wasn't born yesterday and I have a good idea what goes on when all you poets and writers get together."

"What do you mean?"

"OK, I know you took your portable typewriter on that trip but you didn't pack any typing paper at all."

"Come on now, Emily. I didn't want to carry a heavy ream of paper on the airplane when I could buy all I needed right here."

"Yeah? Well, I also know that young impressionable girls fall all over older men when they start poeticizing about limpid eyes, peaches and cream skin tone, and soft as raindrops hair. Who could resist that kind of talk?"

"Emily, I don't go around talking to young girls like that. Anyway, there are no young impressionable girls at this conference."

"Well how about all that boozing it up when you are supposed to be sitting quietly and listening to a lecture?"

"I've only had one cup of coffee. You know I don't drink anything stronger than lemonade."

"And another thing! Is that Pamela Hottotrot also at that conference? Every time I turn around that hussy romance writer is sending you another perfumed letter."

"I don't know . . . well, yes, I think Pamela is here somewhere. But you know we belong to the same poetry club so it's only natural that we write to each other. You really shouldn't let yourself get upset like this just because I enjoy meeting with other writers occasionally."

"You're right, George. Of course you're right and I certainly do trust you. It's just that being separated every year at this time is difficult for me to understand. You know, I don't like all those snooty poets and uppity magazine writers. But I really do trust you, George, so go ahead and have a good time with your intellectual friends. Don't worry about me. I'll stay here at home and take care of the kids."

"Thank you dear. I must hang up now; Pam and Xaviera have invited me to their room to study modern new ways in free verse rhythm in a meaningful stress relationship. So goodbye, dear. It was nice to hear your voice and I'll call you on Friday."

CHAPTER FOURTEEN

Movie stars and million dollar athletes receive tons of fan mail. Writers receive very little fan mail. I once received a letter from Ron Albritton of Wyandott, Michigan. "What kind of man," he asked, "would rather write poetry when there's football and baseball, camping and hiking?" I don't know where he found my name or how he discovered my poetic side but he was apparently sincere in his puzzlement. In short, Ron was questioning my manhood because in his mind real men don't do poetry, just like they don't cook, sew, wash clothes, dry dishes or change baby diapers. I remember once feeling the same way. It was in the fifth grade and Miss Brown was reading to the class from "The Passionate Pilgrim."

"Live with me and be my love
And we will all the pleasures prove
That hills and valleys, dales and fields,
And all the craggy mountains yield.

"There will we sit upon the rocks
And see the shepherds feed their flocks
By shallow rivers, by whose fails
Melodious birds sing madrigals . . . "

The girls sat, some with eyes closed, enraptured by the words and emotion which swept over them from this master poet who somehow seemed to single them out on an individual private basis. The rest of us, being boys, tittered and snickered as we pictured the bard in his high ruffled collars and fancy pantaloons, speaking in a high squeaky voice (or so we imagined) to the courtly ladies about love and romance. Being rough and tough as boys are supposed to be, we shied away from sissified affairs such as poetry, dancing and anything else remotely connected to the soft and weak feminine mystique. We vowed never to grow up and write mushy poems or dance with girls.

Male chauvinists? You bet!

Most people of the masculine gender, young and old, are naturally skeptical of anyone who speaks or writes in words of more than three syllables. We regarded such people as either afraid of getting their clothes dirty or from the other side of town.

It takes only a few years for these ideas to change. In my case, it was high school. In particular — Honey Bun Singletary. She was the sweetheart of Herky High, slender, sylphid, cuddly, with a voice sultry and devastating. Her real name was Eudora but everyone called her Honey Bun because . . . well, because she was the only girl in the sophomore class with a bra size larger than her IQ. She sat across from me in English Lit and the tedious hours of memorizing ancient tortuous poems were more endurable because of her presence. The works of Wordsworth and Tennyson became more enjoyable because Honey Bun liked such things and if she liked them, well I'd just have to like them too.

I poured out my heart to her in short rhyming verses. Each new poem was a continuous unfolding experience. I learned to write couplets with alternating rhyme patterns. Quatrains were followed by tercets, cinquains, octaves and verse narratives. I recognized rhythm and meter as the most basic elements of versification. Trochees, Iambs, and anapests assumed the same level of importance as did Joe Dimaggio, Stan Musial and Ted Williams.

I was addicted!

The more I wrote, the less time I found for hanging out with the guys. Poetry and Honey Bun were rapidly emerging at the top of my list of priorities and my former companions were beginning to look upon me with suspicion. Perhaps I wasn't getting my clothes dirty as often as before but neither was I developing a fondness for cooking or sewing. I hadn't changed that much. My romance with Honey Bun Singletary, however, was not destined for permanence. On our senior trip she ran off with a tour guide from the Smithsonian Museum. I'm sure it was his uniform but she hasn't been seen since.

Meanwhile, my little verses have been published in a number of places so the English Lit classes weren't entirely wasted. Not only that but I'm pleased to say that the guys at Herky High welcomed me back and even closed their eyes whenever I accidentally slipped into words of more than three syllables.

My experience taught me that there is really no reason for guys to fear poetry. It isn't an angry monster at all and many real men were poets. In fact, there is much to be said about the masculinity of other poetic styles. Kipling for instance.

> "... If you can fill the unforgiving minute
> With sixty seconds' worth of distance run,
> Yours is the Earth and everything in it,
> And – which is more – you'll be a Man, my son!"

Let's not forget Ralph Waldo Emerson who wrote about the "shot heard 'round the world" and Tennyson asked that "there be no moaning of the bar, when I put out to sea."

It is the true measure of a man if he can live, dream, think as a man and yet be able to express his love, imagination, and sensitivity so others may know him as a human being. This is best accomplished in the poetry of his soul. What a guy says reveals him as the real man he is and there is no reason for other guys to fear that poetry will rob them of their maleness. A real man can write poetry and he can also cook, sew, wash clothes, dry dishes or change baby diapers. At least, that's what my wife tells me.

As a former contributing editor for Writer's Rescue, I was expected to write an occasional biography of a famous poet or author. Robert Service, Herbert Byron Reece, Robert Herrick, Edna St. Vincent Millay, each in turn fell prey to my pen.

Usually such assignments resulted in side benefits fully unanticipated. My own poetic muse was often goaded, urged, prodded, and otherwise awakened to produce something similar to the styles of my biographic subjects. For instance, while researching the work of Ogden Nash, my muse once more succumbed.

> I swallowed my tongue in apoplexy
> To see the police car I thought was a taxi
> Swing out from the curb as I swiftly drove by
> And fell in behind. "Alas" and "Oh My!"
> I tried to act cool as if nothing occurred
> But somewhere inside, I felt greatly disturbed.
> A glance once or twice in the side rearview mirror
> Confirmed my worst fear. He was drawing much nearer!
> With both hands on the wheel, I eased off the gas
> But he also slowed down. "Why doesn't he pass?"
> Surely there's something he'd rather be doing
> Like chasing bank robbers instead of pursuing
> Innocent people who happened to be
> Obeying the law, like little old me.
> I'll bet he was looking for a trumped-up excuse
> To fulfill his quota for the old calaboose.
> They were probably waiting right then at the jail
> Preparing to laugh at my pitiful tale.
> They've heard it a thousand times over again,
> Whatever I did, it was wrong and a sin
> That I'd live with forever. "I'm sorry!" I cried.
> The police car swept past and I gratefully sighed.
> It took but a moment to recover my nerve
> So I stepped on the pedal and leaned into a curve.
> "Ha!" I exclaimed to none in particular
> But my joy was short-lived; I lost my vehicular!
> I failed to take note of the sharp rounding bend
> And the road I was traveling abruptly did end.
> Oh, it really is nice on this fluffy white cloud.
> I can look down below and be rightfully proud

Of my family and friends. My! There sure is a crowd
All dressed in black suits and mourning aloud.
Yet, somehow I wish it had turned out quite different,
That the obit they published was only a misprint.
But what I really would like is to turn back the time
And be where I was when I started this rhyme.

CHAPTER FIFTEEN

You may have guessed that William Shakespeare has been a favorite target for my little barbed essays. Among his most engaging personal attributes were his courtly demeanor and gentlemanly appearance. The man simply looked and acted like a poet. Well poised and carrying himself with assurance, he was usually bedecked in a moustache with matching goatee and quite macho in a buttoned tunic with billowy sleeves and cape fastened at the neck. Long stockings were in vogue during his era and he wore them with their tops concealed under the folds of pleated pantaloons that terminated about four inches above the knee.

Of course, if old Will was seen in that get-up today in downtown Valdosta, he would surely be the aim of snide remarks and wadded-up Twinkie wrappers. I learned long ago that good ole Georgia boys are naturally suspicious of anyone who wears short pants and speaks in complete sentences. Once, an Ohio couple stopped at Bubba's Texaco for a Co-Cola. They wore flowery Bermudas and must have been homeward bound from Disneyland judging from the Donald Duck decals on their Oldsmobile windshield.

Now, Bubba was located near the Interstate and he was accustomed to seeing tourists on a frequent basis, but on this occasion it so happened that Hank Locklear and Dudley Burnett were there pumping gas into their 4-wheel-drive pickup. When Dudley saw the flowery Bermudas he let out a guffaw and commenced to snigger. Hank told him that it was impolite to snigger but Dudley continued to snigger and to search the ground for a discarded Twinkie wrapper.

The eloquence of Shakespeare in his theatrical plays and sonnets might seem pretentious according to modern standards. Imagine the Bard shopping at Bubba's. "Good morrow sir. Prithee and mayest thou give dalliance while I beseech thee for a tin of yon sustenance?"

"Wachya'llwont?"

"My thoughts I cleave to. I have told thee of it but thy countenance remains stoic and apathetic. Forsooth, look lively sir and dispose thy charge for I am weary and would fain possess that small parcel of powdered preparation for intended application to the nostril."

"Whoa there! Jes a minute, Abner." Turning aside, Bubba would call for assistance. "Cory Mae! C'mere 'n tell me wut this yere Yankee is a-sayin." In our fictional drama, Bubba would have been less than awed upon learning the identity of his customer. To hear him tell it, "Why, I knowed right off the feller was a writer jes by his looks."

Unfortunately, there are some writers who diligently practice the art of assuming the appearance of a writer. Magazine journalists, for instance, project an image of three-piece suits with overcoat casually draped over their left shoulder. News reporters are believed to deliberately purchase rumpled trousers (often with matching jacket). Sports writers smoke black cigars and are forever six hours behind shaving schedule while film scriptwriters brandish pocket watches with ornate good chains. Poets are readily identifiable by thick bushy beards (except for the ladies whose whiskers are barely noticeable). Mystery writers are known by their unbuttoned shirtfronts, and songwriters by baseball caps and their incessant humming.

I never met Hank or Dudley but whenever I stop at Bubba's for a Co-Cola, it's a safe bet that I am wearing my faded blue jeans and Sears-Roebuck shirt. I'll be sporting a baseball cap with "John Deere" prominently displayed across the bill and my eyes are searching the ground for discarded Twinkie wrappers as I drive up to the gas pump in my GMC pickup.

No one yet suspects that I can speak in complete sentences so my secret appears safe for the moment. However, there are some others who recklessly toss complete sentences around willy-nilly without regard for the possible injustice of their actions. I refer to some educators and equal righters who recently alleged that favorite fairy tales such as Snow White and Cinderella are sexist because both story heroines suffered from depression, sorrow and general unfulfillment until a macho prince arrived to save them from their hopeless lot in life. They're even suspicious of old Mother Hubbard who had all those children (probably out of wedlock because no one ever heard of old Father Hubbard).

A Chicago school teacher named Georgianna Carlson is now of the opinion that such tales are demeaning to little girls. She says they grow up feeling inferior and lacking in self-confidence. Consequently, Ms. Carlson is rewriting these stories to give them different endings. In her version, Snow White turns the tables on Prince Charming by rescuing him and then refuses his proposal for marriage. She prefers to live happily ever after as a single woman.

Cinderella also brushes aside her prince for a stable boy or chimney sweep or somebody who doesn't have a coin to his name. I'm not sure what Ms. Carlson has in store for the Hubbard family. Possibly food stamps, AFDC, guidance counseling, a membership in NOW and a one-year supply of contraceptives.

If this sounds like sexism by a male chauvinist, let me ask simply if Ms. Carlson has ever given thought to the downtrodden disadvantaged male heroes of literature. Poor Humpty Dumpty immediately comes to mind. If you recall, he was a good egg but he ate so much of his wife's greasy cooking that he could no longer sit atop a wall without falling off. Furthermore, no one really knows the fate of Jack Sprat, who may have married Humpty's sister-in-law, and how about little Jack Horner? All of these otherwise fine gentleman seemingly had a common failing.

They dearly loved to eat!

But has anyone ever complained that these story characters were wrongfully depicted as typical gluttonous males? What about all the little boys growing up forever being teased by little girls for being roly polys? Is anyone concerned for their undeveloped egos? After all, it was mammas and grandmammas and Auntie Ems who baked all those deep-dish apple pies, spaghetti dinners, and chickens with dumplings.

Ms. Carlson, in her revised story versions, will probably propose that Snow White ate that poisoned apple at the urging of her wicked stepfather, and that it was the King of Hearts who constantly threatened to cut off someone's head. Does the lady from Chicago now intend to alter the empty-headed literary reputations of Miss Muffet, Bo Beep, Red Riding Hood and even Goldilocks while allowing Rip Van Winkle, King Midas, and Wee Willie Winkie to remain without hope of redemption?

The lady Carlson should be alert to the peril of trifling with literary tradition. The changing of old and honored fairy tales would certainly not sit well with the spirits of Robert Louis Stevenson, Lewis Carroll, or the brothers Grimm. Dark and vengeful fables penned amid superstition and belief in witchcraft have been known to come alive and wreak wrathful visits with folk who dared tweak the noses of such immortalized authors.

Walk lightly, Ms. Carlson. Let your pen or word processor be judicious in any reappraisal undertaken under the banner of the liberated woman.

CHAPTER SIXTEEN

Not long ago the world was agog at newspaper accounts of President Reagan and Britain's royal monarch fondly exchanging recitations of Robert W. Service's "The Shooting Of Dan McGrew" and "The Cremation Of Sam McGee." It seems that both Ron and Her Royal Highness are ardent devotés of that English-born Canadian poet.

The London Times questioned, "Does this signal a momentous regression to that bawdy poetic era so personified by Mr. Service?" This editorial further pondered whether the two formidable heads of state also sought to restore dignity to that saucy, impertinent verse that was so well popularized by William Leer, another Englishman ⎯ namely, the limerick.

In the United States critics were gravely apprehensive that a concerted effort may have surfaced to inundate the English-speaking nations of the world with poetry deeply rooted in traditional value. It has since been whispered that the reign of free verse may be at an end and that even now, the modernists are deserting their non-metrical buttresses in droves.

To ascertain the seriousness of this situation, I took it upon myself to locate the eminent H. K. Kniggenfelder, professor emeritus and editor of the National Poetry Chronicle. Mr. K was in residence at a retreat on an undisclosed private estate near Rockingham, in the south of Wales. With some reservation he agreed to be interviewed regarding this matter and the following question and answer session resulted.

Q. Sir, have you read the Times editorial in question?

A. I try my best to avoid any editorial appearing in the Times. However, I must admit having read this one.

Q. What is your reaction to having the poetry of Mr. Service read aloud in the royal palace?

A. Well, let me tell you, I was shocked!

Q. What did you think of the particular two poems involved?

A. I thought them both to be rather in bad taste. After all, the McGrew fellow was a gambler, a drinker and a rogue, while Mr. McGee was a Tennessee Yank. Neither was a proper subject to grace the lips of a gentleman nor a Queen.

Q. How do you account for Her Highness' preference for the somewhat risqué poetry of Mr. Service?

A. Today's customs being what they are, I suggest that Her Majesty was merely being slightly rebellious against the establishment.

Q. But isn't she the establishment?

A. Oh my goodness! So she is. Now you have me rattled.

Q. Since this Service incident, have you noticed whether there has been any noticeable increase in the usage of limericks?

A. Now that you mention it there was one in particular about a young maiden from York who often was courted by dark. Of lovers she had plenty but scruples not any so her most frequent guest was the stork.

Q. Sir. In your opinion, are English and American poets fleeing the nontemporal world of free verse for the limiting constraints and rhythm patterns of traditional rhyming poetry, and is the center of the poetic state being wrested from the avant-garde who are gradually relinquishing their European influence and dominance over Anglo-American poets?

A. Yes.

Q. Are there any abnormal tendencies in your own background?

A. Well, perhaps. But I never wrote an ode about a Grecian urn.

Q. Are you by any chance thinking of switching to the "other" side?

A. Oh No! I was on the other side once before but now I'm on this side.

Q. Professor, before we terminate this interview, is there anything you would like to add concerning the Robert W. Service dilemma?

A. Only this. I wonder if Ron ever got around to reciting The Ballad Of Blasphemous Bill who froze to death and was sheathed in a shroud of white ice gleaming and glittering from head to toe. If you remember, the fellow's body was too large for the makeshift coffin and despite the making of a roaring fire, old Bill could not be thawed . . . or sawed.

'The influence of Robert Service has been felt in the heart and bosom of every novice poet. Certainly in mine. Consider the following.

'This was a tale that was told to bewail the loss of a friend to die. A stranger named Jim beckoned me to him with an offered taste of old red eye and as the liquor burned, this story I learned from old Jim who swore 'twas no lie.

"In fifty-eight the bus was late in our travel to the Golden West. Me and old Ben had just eaten in a diner that was far from best when in through the door of that grimy grease store strode a gal who wasn't all dressed. From her head to her toe all she had she did show and she clearly had brought nothing more. Neither a blush came to cheek nor a word did she speak as she stood there just inside the door. For a moment she waited while the din soon abated, then with purpose she walked 'cross the floor. She seemed not to care that all eyes turned to stare as she surveyed the small room. Without a word said, just a toss of her head and a trace of gardenia perfume, she selected a chair at the next table where a meal she began to consume. It was soon plain to see that all except she were aware of her lack of attire but it seemed no distress that she wore somewhat less than a lady did normally desire. If it hadn't a-been for the paper napkin, her nudity would have been entire."

Now Jim and old Ben were soon taken in by the scene that was displayed before 'em. For the moment at best, they forgot their trek west while the gal continued to ignore 'em. What kept them engrossed and bothered the most was her utterly lack of decorum.

"She continued to eat some fried beans and meat which the owner himself had served her, while the room slowly filled with onlookers who milled about but didn't unnerve her. Then the temperature rose when the gal with no clothes stood up 'til all had observed her. She glanced calmly around the room 'til she found the eyes of old Ben locked upon her. With a voice sultry low and her face full of woe, she asked him to rescue her honor. I knew, oh so plain, when I heard her explain, that my friend was surely a goner.

"Her name was Dolores and she worked in the chorus at the Uptown Macon Dance Hall until the manager's son said she couldn't go on without permitting him a curtain call. When he was denied, he threw reason aside, recalling her act — costumes and all. Now she was (like us) awaiting the Dallas bus for travel to the great Golden West, but after her meal she could no more conceal that she hadn't a dime to invest. And, to compound her worry, she left in such hurry that she barely did note her undress."

Such a simple request (and she *was* heading west) no gentleman could surely refuse. Especially when old Jim and old Ben were alone and had nothing to lose. So after eating her fill, there remained a one-dollar bill for a pair of red velvet shoes. "The shoes," she confessed, "were so she would feel dressed while riding out west in the bus. She'd find something more at a big Dallas store if someone would help her (like us). Until then, she guessed she'd be just as well dressed as could be without any fuss."

So the three of them sat on the hard wooden slats as they waited for the Dallas bus, while gathered around was the whole doggone town, "a-winkin' and a-grinnin' at us." They continued to sit though it chafed them a bit — old Jim, old Ben, and Dolores.

"At a quarter past two the bus rolled into view and the red Georgia dust swirled behind. It was then that old Ben jumped out of his skin when he took out his wallet to find that his ticket was voided for he had avoided the print on the small bottom line.

"Not valid," it read, "unless rider is dead and accompanied by widow, unclothed."

"A small limitation," was Jim's explanation, "and one that should really be loathed but otherwise nice for we discounted the price."

Said Ben, "but I'm not even betrothed!"

With no funds to invest for another trip west, Ben agreed he would lie down and die. And Dolores, though peeved, said that she would be grieved, at least, she would give it a try.

"How lucky!" Ben said, "that I can be dead with friends on whom I can rely."

"And so it was done as the bus rumbled on in our ride to the great Golden West. I sat beside old Ben who had died; a friendship that passed every test. And even Dolores, the girl from the chorus, was dutifully, suitably impressed. Now, I'm all alone and old Ben has gone on to his own private place of renown for he wouldn't awaken, the night we left Macon. He's still riding to some distant town. Dolores, of course, is back in the chorus and she still doesn't own a night gown."

CHAPTER SEVENTEEN

Many writers have found the interview system to be an excellent method of responding to an editor's urgent plea for submission of a column before a deadline. It requires very little thinking and the writer need only converse with himself.

My first published poem appeared in 1973 and since then I have received many requests from scholars seeking the secret of my literary success. For instance, Norbert Richardson, a sophomore at Herky High, wrote and asked my assistance on a Petrarchan sonnet for his English class. Norbert said, "It's due in three weeks but I have football practice four nights a week and on weekends I visit my grandmother in St. Louis." He continued, "I need your response by a week from Monday. Please center the poem, don't underline the title and try not to smudge the paper because neatness counts toward my final grade." The other letter was from Norbert's grandmother inquiring as to the fee I demand from high school students for writing their homework assignments.

I realized there must be countless other fans who would like to ask me questions on the subject of poetry and so I have devised an interview session with myself in an effort to answer the numerous letters which are as yet not received. So without further ado, let's get on with it.

Q. Where do you get your ideas for poems and do you use a nom de plume?

A. That's really two questions but I'll overlook it since I'm the one who's asking. I get some pretty good ideas from Trixie. She's my next-door neighbor and headliner at the Pink Pussycat lounge, but I have never used a nom de plume in my life. I did try a nom de grape once.

Q. Do you write in rhyme or free verse?

A. I usually write in the bathroom and I don't intentionally write free verse. I just seldom get paid for it.

Q. Do you lean toward traditional forms of poetry or are you avant-garde?

A. My old drill Sergeant used to say that I leaned toward lazy. Still, I'm really a modernist where poetry is concerned. I prefer word processors to goose quill pens.

Q. How many hours a day do you work at writing poetry?

A. Only one hour. I spend the rest of the day thinking about it.

Q. Do you take sole credit for your poetry or do you gracefully share honors with your muse?

A. I don't have a muse. I do own a dog and I once had a chicken but it wouldn't catch a ball or give chicken rides, so now I only have a dog.

Q. In summing up, do you have any advice for aspiring poets?

A. No, because I don't believe poets should aspire. If they want to aspire they should become bricklayers or steelworkers. I became a poet because I was tired of aspiring and also having to change my shirt and socks every day.

In addition to interviews, there are also conversations, which serve the same purpose.

Question: Many poets have wondered why neither the New Yorker nor Atlantic Monthly ever publishes one of their poems? The stuff that does appear on the pages of these two highly renowned periodicals seems consistently pretentious and repetitive. I've often thought, like other poets, that my own poetry is certainly as good if not better than what I've read in those two publications. Perhaps there is a conspiracy to deny fame and fortune to poor struggling souls like me.

"Hello! Is this Mike?"

"Yeah, who's this?"

"Hey Mike! It's Pete – from the Atlantic."

"Oh, hi Pete. I'm glad you called. How's the missus?"

"She's fine . . . and your family?"

"Everybody's great here. The baby said her first word and Mikey Junior was just appointed to his high school editorial staff."

"Sounds like a chip off the old block."

"I guess so. Lemme tell you why I called."

"OK. Shoot."

"I just received another batch of poems from that guy down in Georgia."

"You mean he hasn't given up yet?"

"Nope. Looks like some folks never learn, huh?"

"You'd think he'd have wised up by now that we just ain't gonna publish any of his little rhyming verses."

"Ain't that the truth? Ya gotta give him credit for being persistent though."

"You're right about that. Most poets would have given up by now."

"Wonder why he does it. I mean, it's not as if we've encouraged him at all. None of the rejection slips I sent him were even signed."

"Same here. I always gave him the usual excuse. We regret being unable to use your material. Thank you for giving us the opportunity, blah, blah, blah. It's always been good for a chuckle or two."

"Well, we can't really tell him the truth — that no one from Georgia ever wrote anything good except Sidney Lanier and Herbert Byron Reece and they're both dead."

"Yeah, and we didn't publish them either."

"Ha, ha, ha. That's right, so why should we change overnight?"

"Hooo boy! I'm sure glad I called you. It was getting kinda boring over here and I needed a good laugh."

"I know what you mean. It gets tiresome printing the same drivel all the time."

"Yeah, wouldn't it be great to publish something new and fresh for a change?"

"I couldn't agree with you more, but where are all the new imaginative poets of today?"

"Who knows? There just doesn't seem to be any."

"Very true. Although I did see something refreshing in one of those small insignificant publications the other day."

"What was it?"

"It was in a newsletter called Rhyme Time but the name of the poet escapes me."

"Hmmmmh! Maybe we oughta look into that."

"Not a bad idea. We could probably get free copies of it. You know, professional courtesy and all that."

"Let's do it. Anything's better than publishing the same old thing month after month while waiting to discover another Robert Frost in the mail. Say, I wonder if we ever published him."

"Robert who?"

CHAPTER EIGHTEEN

In a previous chapter we discussed strange and eerie voices detected by the antennae systems of writer/poets during certain unguarded moments. Not all of these voices, to be sure, are attributable as helpful whispers of our mythological muses. In illustration, let me point out the occasion when I was walking down Peachtree Street in Atlanta one Sunday night when I suddenly realized my predicament. Nobody walks Peachtree Street at night except out-of-towners, muggers and folks with a strong death wish.

My cautious footsteps led me through a swiftly enveloping mist to an old churchyard where my body gratefully sought a resting place. In my state of distraction I sat upon a marble bench to pause and to gather courage for the long trek back to my hotel. It was then that the whispers began. At first I mistook them for the rustle of oak leaves on a playful breeze that swept past the disarranged grave markers nearby but it was soon evident they were indeed whispers.

Considering the hour and place, I should have been frightened but I was amazed to discover my hands steady and my pulse unaffected as my ears strained to decipher the sibilant murmurs growing ever louder. I scarcely breathed, not wishing to be caught eavesdropping on what was apparently a private discussion between spirits.

"Did you see who was buried today in Potter's Field?" one voice asked.

"No," said another. "I seldom visit there. Was it anyone I knew?"

"It was Jason Longfellow Smith, the famous author."

"Really! I remember him, but why was he buried in Potter's Field? Isn't that area reserved for paupers?"

"Unfortunately, Smith never made any money from his writing. As a matter of fact, there are other writers there also."

"What a shame!" said the first voice. "I wonder why they keep writing their little stories and essays if nobody pays them."

A long pause ensued and I thought the conversation ended until I heard a different voice join in. "Don't you two know anything?" It asked. "Writers don't expect money for their work. They only want to be published and perhaps receive a kind word from historians. Offering money would be an insult to their artistic pride."

"Maybe so," was the reply, "but I think Jason Longfellow Smith would have occasionally liked some cash instead of a kind word."

"Yeah," voice number two agreed, "then at least he could have a headstone with one of his own phrases inscribed on it."

"It's called an epitaph," the newcomer advised. "I'll bet he's written many of those for free."

"Well, it isn't right," said voice number one, "and if I wasn't dead I would do something about it."

"Oh sure! What could you do about it?"

"For one thing, I would buy as many verses and writings as I could."

"There you go again . . . and what would you do with them? You'd have to sell them just to make money so you could buy more and there aren't enough people alive to make it profitable. It's a moot question anyway because you *are* dead and nothing can change that."

Another pause before I heard a faintly offered suggestion. "Well, here's an idea. Inasmuch as we have truly passed beyond the veil, why don't we start our own publishing business? Just imagine how many ghostwriters are lying around here still waiting to be published, never mind the kind words."

"Yes," someone agreed, "and they could all submit their manuscripts directly to the dead letter office."

The chuckling whispers faded into the surrounding mist and I rose from my marble bench to begin my homeward journey. But I was less apprehensive now about walking the street because I had learned of a destiny with much more serious consequences. The hereafter would certainly have to be considered in my future. I must also assure myself of a final resting place far from Potter's Field. Also a stone with my own verse engraved upon it.

As I retraced my steps, I considered the possibility of recognizing those sighing voices at some future time. I would definitely like a word with the fellow who suggested that writers happily forego payment for their work in favor of publication or a kind word.

He was probably a former literary critic.

Many other whispers that we hear are secrets being shared between friends. Secrets they don't wish other people to know. Perhaps an indiscretion or two that would be embarrassing if others became aware of them. We all know, however, that secrets not infrequently have a way of revealing themselves. Writers have their little indiscretions, only a few of which have been bared in the passage of time. Shakespeare is said to have written the first 126 of his sonnets to a young man, possibly a lover but certainly someone of whom he was exceedingly fond. Whatever relationship existed between them shall remain among the shadows for all we have are scattered hints displayed tantalizingly within the sonnets themselves.

Other celebrated writers have been similarly successful in keeping their personal ignominies from the public eye, until now.

Letters were recently discovered in the authenticated handwriting of Percy Bysshe Shelley. It seems that the Shelley household habitually enjoyed dining on gypsy stew and marinated chicken fingers with overnight guests blessed with horrible dreams as a result. Percy continued to crave such delicacies for years afterwards and when he took Mary Godwin for his second wife, she was aghast at the victuals offered at her bridal supper. Dutifully she ate and predictably she suffered but was too embarrassed to complain to her husband. The meals continued as did her frightening nightmares until she decided that Percy should be told.

She couldn't bring herself to speak directly of such evils so she wrote them down for him. Thus was born the tale of the Frankenstein monster.

From diaries and witness statements have come additional revelations concerning some of our most noted poets and authors. Do I dare expose them for what they really are?

Certainly I dare.

Contrary to popular legend, Sir Walter Raleigh did not throw his mantle on the ground for the Queen to walk dry-shod over a puddle, nor did he scribble verses with a diamond on a pane of glass to gain her attention. In reality, he accidentally dropped his kerchief and the Queen stomped on it quite unladylike. He then began writing suggestive limericks to her with a zircon. Likewise, "The Face On The Bar-Room Floor" was not written by H. Antoine D'arcy as literarians contend. It was my brother-in-law's. Not the poem — the face.

And would you believe Emily Dickinson was a swinger who regularly slipped away from home to dance and carouse until dawn? She slept all the next day and awakened to write her little verses until time to party again. No one ever knew about her honky-tonking because she used the pseudonym *Dirty Gertie From Bizerte*.

Walt Whitman defaced more than one public rest room with excerpts from "Leaves Of Grass" and Ezra Pound was christened at birth, Ezra Ounce. No one has ever suspected that William Wordsworth and Henry Wadsworth Longfellow were actually the same person, but should not be confused with Samuel Woodworth who wrote "The Old Oaken Bucket."

Finally, there is the unresolved mystery of O. Henry, an alias used by William Sydney Porter. Rumor has it that Porter originally called himself "O. Butterfinger" for reasons that remain mysterious and baffling.

CHAPTER NINETEEN

Most any quiet Sunday will find me at my writing desk peering at the words I have just written or simply thinking about the words I want to write. It is a time when an abundance of worlds emerge from the shadows of my presumably inactive subconscious mind in a search for a lasting permanence for which only the written word is able to provide.

It is a time when I am united with my personal muse.

Gazing past the shelves of my small library, I often see influences of literary ghosts whose universes have navigated across the gossamer veil of time bearing gifted hints of beauty, adventure, mystery and imagination that somehow failed to find permanence in their own distant lifetime.

I'm sure that such bygone spirits would not mind, in fact they would probably encourage the acceptance of their endowments by poets of this age. Their reasoning being that verses identifiable with any of them would surely accentuate their individual repute. For instance, if a single passage of a modern poem succeeded in evoking some reminiscence of perhaps Longfellow, he (Longfellow) would be better memorialized for it. And today's poet? Well, he might also bask in the reflection of that master poet and be recognized for possessing a similar talent.

I have examined my own published writings and perceived subtle yet clear manifestations of possible literary apparitions. Several essays come to mind wherein their themes betray a supernatural interest in the former lives of favorite poets. In certain instances I have sometimes wondered if my writing was a piece of fiction or did my muse actually achieve an unearthly connection.

It is a common urge for all who engage in the creative pursuits of literature for their writings to endure eternally. One of my earlier poems offered the same thought as shown in the following excerpt.

> "Each private verse that I have penney
> when I was all alone
> Gave comfort much as any friend
> or lover I have known,
> And words appearing on this page
> with auras unconfined
> Perhaps will live beyond my age
> as ghosts I left behind."

Certainly, other poets can observe the awards and honors which they display proudly and are able to trace more than a few of their origins to influences kindled by a word or phrase from the work of a favorite author.

From the vantage of my writing desk, it is possible to imagine the machinations of kindred spirits vying for control of a writing hand in a spectral struggle to achieve literary permanence. A number of poems and adventure tales undoubtedly are yet unwritten but still flitting about in the murky caverns of subconscious worlds. It needs only a receptive and imaginative mind to detect and extract the wealth available from this shadowy realm.

Consequently, the thoughtful contemplations of a writer conceivably could extend beyond the mere selection of an exact word or phrase for his current project. He too may be one with his muse, who may be conducting a search of its own.

Before writers blamed everything on their personal muses, living used to be so simple. In my case it was rise before daybreak, feed the chickens, slop the hogs, and stay out of Mr. Winheim's cherry trees. It was those cherry trees more than anything else that gave my backside a firm relationship with my father's old army garrison belt.

Mr. Winheim was our neighbor back in Missouri and his cherry trees were a boy's dream. Their deep red complexion and sweet taste were lures I simply could not ignore. Their branches were sturdy and grew close together, making it perfect for escaping from wild toothy tigers or a charging rhinoceros. They also served as a crow's nest on Blackbeard's pirate ship, a parlor for Tarzan, and a meeting place for secret agents.

Today the cherry trees are gone. They were replaced by inanimate brick and siding in a subdivision known as "Cherry Acres." The eventual ruination of that orchard makes me wonder about other treasures of the past and whether they also surrendered to the urgencies and demands of civilization. Is this what actually happened to the dinosaur? Were the divinities of Mount Olympus relegated to mythology as an aftermath of human intrusion? What do we really know about Atlantis? All that has survived from bygone eras is in the recorded words of buried generations. Even the oceans and mountains are not as they once were.

Our legacy has descended to us in the words of Socrates, Aristotle, Pindar, Michelangelo, Leonardo da Vinci, Chaucer and Lincoln. The list is endless. It remains for voices of the present to perpetuate such treasures for generations yet to come and whether they speak in poetry, song, philosophy, history, art, science, government, exploration, or commerce. Living in tomorrow's world will undoubtedly be more sophisticated than we may imagine and our own simplicities may become subjects of museum exhibition. But it is our words that the future is dependent upon.

Poetry may be likened to a window through which may be seen the soul of humanity. It is also a key to living and the mother of accomplishment. Above all, poetry is a bridge constructed with bricks of verse, stone of imagery, and mortar of eloquence; a bridge permitting access into parallel worlds of adventure, romance, reverie and inspiration ⁻ worlds in which there is truly something of value for all who cross.

The many poets and writers who labored in building this bridge have been continually striving to improve and strengthen its structure by new creations that excite the senses and inflame the passions. Their words are yet vibrantly alive, emotionally stirring, hauntingly eerie, and enchanting in sheer honesty and sincerity. By their own hands they placed each brick with care so the bridge would endure. The mortar was applied with skill that the journey would become as pleasurable as the visit across the river of dreams.

There have been innumerable builders since construction of the bridge began. Their individual identities have not all survived the ravages of time and some preferred their personal contributions to remain anonymous. Yet, they were all instrumental in inching civilization up the cultural ladder by introducing aesthetic enjoyment in song and prose. The bridge was slowly embellished as a result of their inherent sensitivity to innermost sensations of their fellow man and by their own mastery of the tools of language.

Each parallel world connected by the bridge is complete unto itself with seas and lands reflecting the mood of each pensive traveler. Within the world of Romance are lofty mountains of emotion and foothills that are blessed with placing lakes of blue fidelity. In the world of Adventure are tunnels burrowing deep below the surface and darkened with strange fears and eerie delights. The world of Reverie boasts gentle breezes to caress the memory and soothe anxious hearts. In the world of Inspiration are transparent oceans of divine exaltation, sandy shores abundant with self-confidence, and verdant forests resplendent with the spirit of brotherly love.

But, let us imagine for a moment that our bridge had not been conceived. Let us pretend it was never constructed because of a critical absence of builders. If this were true, we would now be aware only of our own peripheral existence and would not have reaped benefits of such notable builders as Homer, Virgil, Dante, Shakespeare, Spencer, Burns, Keats, Byron, Kipling, Longfellow, Wordsworth, Poe, Dickinson or Frost.

Without the bridge there would be no parallel worlds. Consequently, we would not have discovered the beauty of nature nor would there be any real meaning to our observance of a new day dawning, the chirp of a robin, lovers strolling in the moonlight, or a private talk with God. Let us then be grateful for all the builders who have served to renovate our bridge throughout eras of history and to ensure an open passage for travelers to each of the parallel worlds.

It eventually becomes our privilege to contribute our own labors to the perpetuation of the bridge. However, lest our limited talents prove inadequate to excite the senses or inflame the passions, travelers should be cautioned that our bricks are new, our stones are uncertain, and our mortar is experimental.

CHAPTER TWENTY

Angela wilted in his arms as his lips traced a line from her soft cheek down to her lovely neck. She felt his strong hand caress the swelling of her breast and she knew that she could never refuse him . . .

New writers are often embarrassed about the apparent necessity of explicit sex in modern romance novels. Writing about love as an act of passion should be exciting for the author as well as for the intended reader. But it doesn't have to be a modest red-faced shameful experience for either unless it is a deliberate marketing requirement.

Like most women, my mother devoured Harlequin romance novels because she fervently believed all stories should have happy endings and that love conquers all. Harlequin comes closer to fulfilling that old adage than do many other publishers of romantic fiction. Why is this? Perhaps because Harlequin insists that their authors treat romantic sensual interludes with respect rather than presenting lessons in anatomy or tawdry graphic displays of pure unadulterated s e x.

The literary definition of this genre has seemingly undergone a subtle alteration from old-fashioned amorous suspense in favor of erotic lust. This change is arguably the result of telling it like it is, earthy and wantonly crude rather than storytelling in the manner of Victorian romance authors.

More than a few publishers thrive on bold uninhibited stories of free love and nonstop sex, especially if amplified by lurid and suggestive photographs that leave nothing to the imagination. These markets are eager for adventures of sexual encounters and often pay handsomely for them. However, if you, as a writer, are more interested in writing about romance spelled with a capital "R," then be assured that there is also a marketplace for you.

Editors of romance and confession magazines offer suggestions regarding their preferences in submitting fiction for their readers' pleasure. Their overall mood seems to say transmit your dreamiest and most imaginative sensual story and save your lewd sleazy tales for the hardcore porno trade. They caution, however, to make sure the story is written in a style that would entice their particular readers into buying it. And payment is pretty good in this market too.

There is no denying that truly romantic adventures are written with the female viewpoint in mind. Women comprise the largest group of buyers of love stories while it is the male reader who is more likely to purchase the sexual fantasies.

Much has been said about the lascivious nature of the male specie. In particular, the old geezers who sit on park benches ogling the young ladies passing by and perhaps imagining the various charms of each. I would like to intervene at this point on behalf of the old geezers in this world. By virtue of their advanced age, they have earned the right to sit on that bench and to dream their wistful dreams. Such ogling may be likened to the admiration of a lovely painting. The texture of each brush stroke employed by the artist is readily apparent and it's easy to appreciate the softness and boldness of the overall image. Nevertheless, should that painting be presented to the old man sitting on the park bench, chances are he wouldn't know what to do with it. It's pretty much the same thing with ogling. However, ogling is not a venue strictly reserved for old geezers. The young geezers enjoy it too.

The skills and techniques used in writing tales of romance are similar as for writing confession stories. The difference being that confessions are usually written in the first person and bylines are not used to identify the author. As with any other type of fiction, quality plots with good grammar and language usage will always sell.

One of the complaints most often uttered by writers is they can't seem to write about love without getting their heroine into bed. Fortunately, or unfortunately depending on the story angle, sex is not always the intended goal of writing romantic adventures. The old movie theme of boy sees girl, boy wants girl, and boy gets girl is no longer good enough. Now, it's girl wants boy, misunderstanding causes girl to lose boy, problem is solved, and girl gets boy. Even when sex is the intended object, the how of it can be more interesting and more readable than the doing of it. The same goes for the dialogue. Vulgar "street" language is best reserved for those publications that concentrate on male viewpoints. Yet, the romance writer can duplicate the situations and characterizations while still avoiding the objectionable. For practical purposes, identical stories can be created for Harlequin and Hustler, for example, simply by altering the dialogue and language expressed in each version.

Authors of romance have the option of deciding whether the sex in their stories will result from love or lust but writers of sexual fantasy have no such option. Sex may be skillfully implied by the one but must be illustratively displayed by the other. Of course, all muses get carried away at times and writers must exercise strict control in enforcing the guidelines of their predetermined story plot.

It is important to acknowledge up front that all writing is commercial and the successful writer is one who not only has developed a style most comfortable for them but one having a quality that commands respect from editors and readers alike. The big question then is whether the story is about love or sex. Writers with difficulty in understanding if their love scenes fall into either group should apply the *blushing mother test* to their finished manuscript. Passing or failing this test will determine which market to pursue.

Writers who approach editors with a fresh story plot always find that the door to publication is forever open but there are times when plots refuse to develop. Many writers have learned that there is an art to writing when it is impossible to think of anything to write about. There is no secret to it, no gnashing of teeth to get it done and no summoning of spirits for inspiration. The initial step is simply to decide what *not* to write about. The choice then becomes a process of elimination.

The first subject that I generally eliminate is sex. I seldom write about it because my close acquaintances wouldn't believe I know much about it anyway and there are others with the opinion that whatever I wrote about sex would probably be copied from someone else. Actually, I don't like to write about sex because I get so worked up that my glasses fog over and I can't locate the proper keys on my keyboard. So, I seldom write about sex.

Another topic that I don't write about is politics. Everyone has their own thoughts about politics and nothing I could say would influence them to change their ideas, ill-perceived as they may be. All right, so I did pick Dukakis to win in 1984.

A writer should maintain absolute objectivity concerning religion, which is another subject that I avoid writing about. I am not a fanatic about it but my personal belief is that religion is a matter between me and . . . well, it's a private matter. Some folks talk to God while others talk to trees or the sun. One of these days we will all know who is right and who will go where.

Often when I am searching for things not to write about, it occurs to me that many famous writers have used this identical formula in furthering their ambitions or to acquire their daily bread. Cleopatra, for instance, never wrote about snakes in her torrid love letters to Marc Antony. If she had, he might have become less infatuated with her and more concerned with his Roman duties. He might then have avoided his eventual downfall and Cleo could have eluded the fateful asp.

One of the most prolific writers of our time was H. Allen Smith, author of "Low Man On A Totem Pole" and other literary classics. Mr. Smith was a master of the writing profession and his books were liberally sprinkled with personal vignettes that were absolutely spellbinding in their narration. He studiously avoided writing about sex, politics and religion.

In addition to not writing about sex, politics, and religion, I also try not to write about morbid things such as Asian wars, dieting, or the scarcity of Tootsietoys from Hong Kong. This leaves me totally free to write about dogs, children, wives, movies, brothers-in-law, old cars, space travel, and the San Diego Padres. Whenever my mind draws a temporary blank and a deadline fast approaches, I combat the foreboding anxiety of near panic by asking myself, "What do I feel like not writing about today?" If my reply fits one of the ostracized categories, I repeat the question until a suitable topic is selected and before I know it, the essay or article has been written.

Just like here and now.

CHAPTER TWENTY-ONE

One reason why I almost always wanted to be a writer was to create fairyland people. The creation of any kind of fictional character is sort of godlike but folks who live in make-believe land are somehow special because they lead such interesting lives. Of course, fairy tales are very close to being real. Consider Wilbur Lovelylocks, the poet.

Once upon a time in a land far away, there lived a beautiful princess who was loved fervently but alas, futilely by Wilbur Lovelylocks, a brilliant albeit impoverished vendor of rhyme. It was Wilbur's misfortune that circumstances presented him with a flair for lyrical poetry, a career dangerously near the poverty level. He was thus unable to attire himself in golden raiment or to possess handsome gifts with which to pursue a proper courtship of the fair and quite unattainable Princess Leana. He could only worship from afar and pen his sad sonnets of affection.

One day, who should appear at Wilbur's Ye Olde Poetry Shoppe but the sinister and black hearted Prince Hugo de Stinker. Hideous to gaze upon, the Prince was also feared as an evil sorcerer. He openly vowed to woo Princess Leana and make her his bride. Toward this purpose he sought to hire Wilbur to create a love poem.

Wilbur found himself in a quandary. Dare he refuse and incur the wrath of the villainous Prince or should he exercise professional objectivity and strive for perfection in the creation of a love poem for his rival to claim as his own? On one hand he risked his bardic honor — on the other, he gambled the loss of his secret love forever. With reluctance born in the reality of his lowly position, he accepted the poetic commission and his melancholy heart proceeded to dictate a poem of forlorn love.

Wilbur abandoned himself in his lonely room where he labored for days into weeks and weeks into months. The power of his love for the Princess filled his soul and guided his hand in the deft formation of words and phrases designed to capture the fluttering heart of any maiden. Finally one dawn found Wilbur slumped over his desk, eyes closed in weary slumber, goose quill pen in hand.

His task completed.

Now it happened that Leana's father, King Gudhart, was getting on in years and he worried about having no sons to carry on the family business. He decided that any son-in-law was preferable to no son at all and so he devised a competition whereby eligible bachelors would vie for the hand of his lovely daughter.

Announcements circulated throughout the kingdom urging all contenders to sign up for the Royal tourney scheduled to commence within a fortnight. As the date of competition neared, the King was perplexed because only Prince Hugo had enrolled as a contestant.

"I do not understand," said the King. "Surely there are other young men willing to compete for my daughter and for the throne." He was unaware that Prince Hugo had threatened to transform anyone who signed the contest register into a loathsome frog.

On the day before the contest, the Prince returned to Wilbur's Poetry Shoppe for his love poem. It was then that Wilbur learned of the competition and that no one yet dared to challenge the Prince. Wilbur had to find a way to enter the tournament. "Would it not be better for your image, oh Prince," he inquired, "if you actually won the contest rather than being awarded the prize by default?"

Prince Hugo mused for a moment and replied, "Perhaps you are right. There will be time enough to turn subjects into frogs after I am king." He stroked his chin and thought aloud, "but where shall I find someone at this late date to compete against me? Everyone has been frightened away."

Wilbur held his breath and scarcely dared to hope.

"Of course!" the Prince exclaimed. "You, poet! You will oppose me in the contest. However," he warned with a wicked leer, "you better make it look good or I'll turn you into a frog."

And so began the competition amid the blare of silver trumpets and before thousands of awed spectators. The palace was bedecked with banners and from each turreted spire flew ribboned flags of neighboring kingdoms whose citizens traveled long distances to witness the event.

Wilbur and the Prince stood side by side as King Gudhart and Princess Leana entered the arena. The King extended his imperial greetings to the impassioned throng and then detailed the activities to follow. Neither adversary had been advised concerning specific events of the tournament in which they would soon participate. The Prince, however, came fully prepared in a camisole of iron mail and a shiny new broadsword forged from the finest Carpathian process of metallurgy. Wilbur seemed frail by comparison as he stood unarmed in a linen tunic gathered loosely at the waist and adorned by a thin cloth sash.

The first match was to determine the stronger of the two and it was no surprise when the Prince won handily. A foot race was scheduled next but Wilbur was hopelessly outdistanced by the longer legs of his opponent.

Two to nothing was the score.

A third contest measured their artistic talents. They were each required to sing a popular song while accompanying themselves on a musical instrument. The gravelly voice of Prince Hugo was not equal to the melodious tenor tones of Wilbur's soft rhapsodic ballad or his dexterous strumming of the lyre.

The Prince frowned but said not a word.

An ominous silence filled the arena as attendants then brought forth two sparrows, each with a broken wing. The first sparrow was handed to the Prince who examined the bird carefully and, noting it was in extreme pain, swiftly slew it to end its suffering. The other sparrow was presented to Wilbur who devised a splint for its injured wing and placed it on a matted cushion fashioned from tufts of dried grass. He then gently laid the bird on the ground before him.

It was announced that this test of compassion was a victory for Wilbur. The tournament was tied! Anger masked the Prince's face. "Poet, you have defied me and for that I will turn you into a frog."

"Wait!" Wilbur shouted. "In your own words you commanded me to make the contest look good. How can you now turn me into a frog for following your instructions?"

"You're right, but don't make the mistake of thinking you can win this competition by trickery." Prince Hugo was yet a viperous enemy.

"This will be the final event," intoned the King.

Wilbur knew he had to outwit the diabolic Prince but how could he do it and escape the certain magic spell that would transform him into a frog?

The King continued. "To show his love for my daughter, each contestant shall write a love poem for which she will be the judge."

Wilbur's heart sank in despair. How could he create a love poem to surpass the one he had previously sold to Prince Hugo? That poem was his greatest creation. It was not possible to compose one better. Sadly he stood and watched as the Prince advanced toward the Royal viewing stand and commenced to read aloud the words, which unknown to anyone else, bespoke of Wilbur's love for the beautiful Princess Leana.

Then a strange thing happened. As the Prince recited the tender poetic phrases, twitters and snickers were heard from the listening multitude for the espoused vows of love, honor, and fidelity were so uncharacteristic of the despicable Prince that they were fully unbelievable. It was evident to all the spectators that the words of this poem were not truly his. The sound of derisive laughter grew so loud that the Prince hesitated, sputtered in confusion, and finally ceased reading altogether. Now the throng quieted in electric anticipation, fearing the wrath of this vile wizard who delighted in transforming people into frogs. When the Prince halted his recitation, King Gudhart rose to challenge him.

"Prince Hugo de Stinker," he formally addressed him. "Is it a certainty that you have perpetrated a fraud and that you are not the author of the poem you entered in this competition?"

The Prince scowled because his subterfuge had been publicly unmasked but he had no choice except to admit the charges were truthful. He was therefore banished immediately from the kingdom forever, an act that also stripped him of all his magical powers. The King embraced Wilbur and Princess Leana, declaring them betrothed.

And the moral of this story is — don't ever open a poetry shoppe unless you have a rich wife who will permit you to be King of her castle.

CHAPTER TWENTY-TWO

Alfred's mother warned him not to marry Alice. Not that she wasn't a pretty girl because she certainly was all of that. Neither was it because she wasn't sweet and loving. No, the reason went much deeper. A sad case really because, you see, Alice was a writer and therein lay the problem as Alfred's mother saw it.

Nevertheless, they were married but there was no honeymoon. Oh, they went to Niagara Falls like other newlyweds but Alice informed her new husband that she was working night and day on a fiction novel and her deadline was just seven days away. "I knew you'd understand, honey," she told him.

Albert did understand. He enjoyed the grandeur and beauty of the falls while his bride completed Chapter Eight. He photographed the International Bridge and purchased souvenirs at Queen Victoria Park as Alice spent the day on authenticity research and half the night rewriting Chapter Twelve. Albert rode the elevator alone to the foot of the falls and visited the Cave of the Winds behind the curtain of falling water. He mailed funny post cards to friends back home and played solitaire while Alice put the finishing touches on her novel just in time to meet her deadline. Of course, that was also the day they had to depart for home. But Albert understood.

Albert recognized early in his marriage that his new bride possessed a consuming desire to write. It may have been the night she brought her typewriter to bed so she could work on an article for Woman's Day. Her passion for the written word was rather embarrassing at times and Albert had to explain to the neighbors more than once why their bedroom lights remained on throughout the night. They finally converted the dining room into an office complete with filing cabinet, portable bookshelves, fax machine and modem for the new computer.

Perhaps Albert recalled his mother's warning more than once and maybe he did experience an occasional twinge of remorse because there were times when their relationship was slightly less than idyllic. For instance, for two weeks in February they scarcely saw each other. Well, to be more exact, Albert saw her but she was entirely oblivious to him.

As with most novelists, Alice became totally committed to whatever project she happened to be involved in and so she routinely tuned out everything except the drama unfolding at her keyboard. During those two weeks she was unfeeling, unseeing, uncaring, and nothing existed outside her own creative mind. She could easily have starved to death while resolving her murder mystery or extricating her protagonist from the clutches of a heinous villain

Albert tried many ruses to distract her concentration long enough for her to consume a sandwich and glass of milk. He passed notes before her eyes advising that their children had been kidnapped and were being held for ransom. He exclaimed that her own mother was at that moment giving birth to quintuplets and that a horse was taking up residence in the kitchen. All to no avail. He then simulated a house fire through the use of a smudge pot billowing black smoke into her dining room office, after which he rushed in and carried her off to safety.

Once, he succeeded in spiriting her away to the seashore for a much needed respite and she gave no outward indication of grief for having to leave her work behind. She appeared to enjoy basking on the sand in the warm Florida sunshine and Albert began to nurture a bit of hope that she would yet be capable of leading a normal life. Such sentiment was soon dispelled for although she pretended to relish the healing rays of the sun and the warm gentle breezes of the Caribbean, Alice was surreptitiously writing poetry in the sand with her index finger.

Albert finally accepted his fate. No more did he attempt to dissuade his wife from her addictive writing compulsion. The most comforting thought he now had is that Alice seemed quite happy in her state of suffering. She really was a loving and devoted wife, when between writing projects. Besides, the few bucks she occasionally received wasn't hard to take either.

Alice, like all writers, used to have a life before she decided to pursue the written word. It's difficult for some people to realize that things were not always the same as in this modern high-tech world. My own children often ask, "Daddy, what did you do in the old days, you know, before TV?"

As I think back I seem to remember playing outside a lot. Baseball, kick the can, tag, hide and seek. When we had to stay in the house because of bad weather, for instance, we played Monopoly or checkers. We read books and listened to the radio. "You sat around and listened to the radio?" They could not believe such a thing. How can we expect them to understand life in that prehistoric age? It's as difficult for me to comprehend how my parents managed to survive without electricity or a telephone.

I never felt deprived for not having a stereo or television during my growing up years. A person cannot feel deprived for not having things that are yet to be invented. I never heard of television back then but it wouldn't have mattered because I had books to read and of course, the magic of radio.

Radio was truly an enchanting device because it stimulated the imagination of each listener. There must have been a million people absorbed in the weekly adventures of Doc and Reggie in I Love A Mystery. Listeners used their powers of imagination to see each scene differently. Individual fantasies were influenced by sound effects and dramatic readings from hand-held scripts. We were not limited in our interpretation of a story line but were free to experience the depth of any scene based only on what we heard.

Afternoons were filled with stirring tales of Terry And The Pirates or Smiling Jack Martin matching wits with smugglers. I could close my eyes and accompany Buck Rogers to the 25th century or thrill to Jack Armstrong, the all-American boy.

Afterwards I could decode the latest message on my Dick Tracy secret crimebuster decoder. After supper, the family gathered around the Philco to await the sound of Inner Sanctum's squeaking door followed by true escapades of Gangbusters. We laughed at Baby Snooks, George and Gracie, Charlie McCarthy and Mortimer Snerd, and the whimsies of Fibber McGee and Molly. As for the cinema, once a week we attended the latest Hollywood movie without leaving our living room simply by tuning in the Lux Radio Theater.

Whenever a slight fever or tummy ache kept me home from school, I enjoyed the stories of Ma Perkins and Aunt Jenny, and I will never forget the burning question posed daily of Our Gal Sunday: *Will the girl from the little mining town of Silver Creek, Colorado, find love and happiness as the wife of the wealthy and handsome Lord Henry Brinthrop?*

Today, as I observe my grandchildren sitting in front of the TV to watch the Flintstones, Pink Panther, Spider Man or Hulk Hogan in all their glory and in full color, I can't help but wonder whatever happened to my boyhood heroes, those dinosaurs from another time. And I speculate as to whether Buck Rogers survived the 25th Century or if Sunday is still married to that English fella!

CHAPTER TWENTY-THREE

Most poets cease writing in rhyme after the initial thrill of being published wears off. Before reaching that point, they may be observed walking around with a glazed expression and distant look in their eyes . . . mesmerized by the sorcery of sound.

I was no exception.

"What are you doing?" my father asked.

"I'm trying to think of a word to rhyme with chilblain."

"Well, how about migraine, which is what you give me whenever I see you stalking throughout the house like a zombie?" His dream of my becoming a doctor or plumber had long passed the point of no return.

Dabbling in rhyme is a craving much the same as gambling or swimming nude in a backwoods creek. A necessity for young lovers and outhouse versifiers, it is yet frustrating because rhyme is suspected of being somewhat less than serious poetry. To some, rhyme fails to possess the freedom and irregular rhythms of speech or prose.

"So, you're a poet!" someone remarks. "What kind of poems do you write?"

"Oh, I write free verse."

How could I openly admit to writing poetry that has no arrangement of rhyme, no poignant tone? How could I possibly accept that all the master poets before my time were all writers of inferior verse? It has been my experience that writing rhymes is fun, almost as much fun as skipping flat rocks across a cow pond by moonlight.

"Hey, Eddie! Wha'cha doing tonight?"
"Gonna skip some rocks across the pond. Wanna come?"
"No thanks. I'd rather stay home and write some rhymes."

The function of rhyme is to accent the emotional quality of a poem. Accomplished poets make use of rhyme as an artistic resource binding their lines together in a delightful pattern that etches them in memory. Rhyming has long been an important part of the technique of poetic expression. It is a mystery then, why ultra modern poets tend to regard it as comparatively trivial. Poetic appreciation is a matter of individual preference but no one seems to know exactly what poetry is. It has been variously called a creation of beauty in words, emotion in musical form, a marriage of pleasure and truth.

Many believe all poetry should possess the traditional enchantments of rhyme and meter. Some insist that old ways must make room for new while others claim that new ways can include the old, and if all this sounds like straddling the fence, that's exactly what it is. But there is no room for exclusivity among today's poets. It is important for the neophyte to experience the basic musical elements of poetry before progressing to more complicated free verse forms and beyond. Consequently, it is most difficult to avoid the confusion of modern verse structure without first serving an elemental apprenticeship in traditional rhyming forms of poetry.

A few extremists contend that it is necessary for artists, whether painters, poets or novelists to suffer in order to succeed. Most of us disagree, however, that success is achieved only through torturous experiences. If that were true it would naturally follow that the more suffering endured . . . the more success secured.

Being spurned by readers or an editor can understandably cause anguish and heartache to a writer's ego. It is painful and agonizing but not unique and certainly not a hurdle that cannot be overcome. The reasons for rejection are many and diverse but serious writers accept them as personal challenges and turn them to their own profit. This may be best realized by exchanging the author's cap for one that reads "Editor" whenever a manuscript returns unwanted. A logical period of mourning, if followed immediately by an impersonal review, will often confirm fatal errors in the manuscript plot or dialogue and even reveal grammatical miscues not evident during the previous rush of submission.

Much has been said regarding the process of transforming an amateur wordsmith into an accomplished author or at least into one who attains publication on a semi-regular basis. Time is the usual catalyst that makes this happen while frustration should be recognized as merely a temporary distraction. A writer will either muddle through such trials with determination or fall by the wayside.

Budding writers should realize that writing is not fun. It's damn hard work and I defy anyone to deny it. Short fiction is somehow more difficult to write than are novels, notwithstanding the insight of a well-known writer who once proclaimed that "the only difference between short fiction and a novel is the comparative length of each." Yet, we can all take heart in the words of Carl Van Doren, a noted writer and editor, who commented that "Yes, it is hard to write, but it's harder not to."

Constructing a story means following the same rules as writing anything else. There is a beginning, a middle, and an ending. Many writers raise their pens or position their keyboards to immediately begin the process of exchanging thoughts and ideas into words and phrases for prospective readers. Others contemplate for long time periods before addressing the work at hand. Regardless which system is used, words, sentences, and paragraphs are duly formed into coherent sequences much as an adventure is molded, shaped, and polished into a finished literary product. The most difficult task is to consider unfavorable criticism at face value without a degree of hurt because someone "out there" isn't fond of what the writer has written.

The best advice I ever received along these lines came in the form of a rejection slip, pre-printed and indifferent as the telephone company's yellow pages. This one had the usual listed reasons why my manuscript was not acceptable. A penciled "X" denoted which excuse best applied but this particular editor took extra time to offer a brief comment.

"There was no poetry in your story," he said.

A quick reassessment of my rejected manuscript revealed grammatically correct sentences and a plot that appeared to move smoothly from page to page. So what was that editor talking about? Only after the third reading did I finally concede that my story indeed lacked some of the simplest devices employed in the creation of a poem. Without my knowledge and behind my back, my muse had been magically transported from poetry into the world of fiction without remembering that similar rules were applicable to both. I had to admit there was no poetry in my story due to the absence of metaphor, simile, alliteration, assonance, etc.

The art of putting poetry into fiction has been accomplished in varying degrees by novelists and short story authors with equal success. Poe was a master of integrating poetic devices within the framework of his fiction and they served him well in arousing the imagination while enthralling readers in each chapter. Let's look at what he said in "The Premature Burial."

"To be buried while alive is, beyond question, the most terrific of these extremes which has ever fallen to the lot of mere mortality. That it has frequently, very frequently, so fallen will scarcely be denied by those who think. The boundaries, which divide Life from Death are at best shadowy and vague. Who shall say where the one ends, and where the other begins?"

According to Poe, certain themes are fully absorbing and readers of fiction experience them with a thrill and the most intense pleasurable pain. Premature burial was such a theme.

CHAPTER TWENTY-FOUR

Contrary to popular belief, happiness is not a warm puppy. It is neither a bouquet of roses nor an annual bonus at Christmas time. It isn't even having your back scratched or your tummy rubbed. Do I speak sacrilege? Are these un-American remarks? No, I think not.

"All right then," you may ask. "What is happiness?"

Are you ready? OK. Pure sugarcoated, blue-ticked, honest-to-Pete happiness is winning poetry contests.

Hah! Don't scoff. You know it's true. Otherwise, why do you clatter away on that antique typewriter in your little corner of the house? Why do you wear those outlandish earmuffs to screen out the sound of your 16-year-old future rock star's 150-watt Peavey studio amplifier as you put the finishing touches on that sonnet for Midwest Poetry Review?

You want to be famous? You want to be immortalized with the likes of Shelley, Keats, and McKuen? Of course you do. Well, I can help you attain those goals because I have participated in all the poetry contests advertised in Writer's Digest and I have learned the secret of winning. So, if you're thinking of entering the world of poetry winners, there are ten rules that, if followed, will go a long way toward bestowing upon you the distinction of being an award-winning poet.

(1). Write your poem entry on the back of an envelope or on a paper napkin. Judges will conclude that your verse was immaculately conceived without need for revision.

(2). Don't bother with strict rhyming schemes or patterns. If you cannot think of the right word to use, invent one. You will be given credit for extra effort.

(3). Use naughty four-letter words throughout your poem and you will certainly gain the Judge's attention.

(4). Repeating a word or phrase over and over repetitiously in a redundant manner is an unusual technique and is certain to be noticed. Remember, if you come up with something good, use it again and again and again.

(5). Don't beat around the bush. If you have something to say, say it. Judges don't want to have to guess what your poem is about. They aren't kids anymore and they need all the help you can give them.

(6). Always observe deadlines. Make sure your entry is received on the last day of eligibility. Judging usually begins as the first poem is received. So, if your poem is read last, it will be the easiest to remember.

(7). Enter the same poem in several contests simultaneously so you will have a better chance of winning. It is important, however, to keep this confidential until you have been awarded your prize.

(8). Copy someone else's poem and enter it as your own. Chances are it will never be questioned but if it is, simply withdraw it with an air of innocence and apologize profusely.

(9). Demonstrate your poetic knowledge by using clichés, adjectives, and foreign words. Dazzle 'em with footwork. Use tried and true metaphors and never attempt anything new or different that could possibly be misunderstood.

(10). Always accompany your entry with a long cover letter containing conversational chit-chat so the contest editor will feel that he knows you intimately. You should include a listing of numerous prestigious awards that you have previously won. (You may have to hedge a little here). Judges are easily impressed by past accomplishments and will surely give you preference over some nobody.

    Let me assure you that I have no ulterior motive in sharing these rules even though we may be competitors from time to time. For the best results, I suggest you clip them out and tape them to the wall directly in front of your trusty old typewriter or computer so they will always be available as a ready reference guide.

    If, after following these rules, your poems are still rejected or, as in some instances not even returned, it is probably the editor's fault. Editors offer numerous excuses for not accepting submissions of well-written poems but let's look at some of the real reasons for editorial rejections.

- ? Darn that Postal Service!
- ? We're hoping for a speedy resolution of the printer's strike.
- ? What entry? Uh, oh!
- ? We were attacked by a big hungry bear and had to feed him *something*.
- ? Almost all of your entry was recovered from the fire.
- ? Sorry, but our Chief Editor is still on vacation.
- ? Be patient! We're not through throwing darts at it yet.
- ? Do you realize what spilled coffee can do to cheap paper?
- ? It's given us our best laugh in months.
- ? Have you tried the poet's help line? Call 1-800-555-OOPS.

CHAPTER TWENTY-FIVE

Would you believe that I, of all people, among the teeming millions of American citizens, some possibly more deserving, should be nominated for the honor of Man Of The Year?

Yet, it happened.

The letter arrived by regular mail from North Carolina and the words contained therein are forever engraved in my heart; *selected by the International Board of Research, exceptional honor, elegant proclamation, great achievement, esteemed standing within society.*

I was thrilled beyond expectation and yet mystified as to what outstanding feat I may have accomplished to gain such recognition? Perhaps it was some remarkable humanitarian act to which I paid little attention at the time. I am always doing things like that. Or maybe it was the letter I wrote to the editor of the Atlanta Journal-Constitution about my proposed slogan for increasing tourism. "Keep Georgia Green – Bring Money." On second thought, the editor's response to that was not very complimentary. So what could I have done to achieve an esteemed standing within society? Well, I did serve on the Doraville Little League Board Of Directors until someone learned it was my vote that opened the door for girls to play baseball with the boys. Society is still trying to cope with that situation.

It's really quite an enigma as to why the International Board of Research singled me out for this prestigious award but I'll just add it to all the other honors for which I have been nominated in recent years by this same eminent aggregation. Let's see now. There was Who's Who in America, Great Men of our Time, Distinctive Poets of the Century, and The World's Most Significant Idols.

No doubt I belong in all those categories. However, there is a slight possibility that something is not exactly kosher here. I have detected a faintly perceptive pattern to these nominations. For one thing, the International Board of Research is based, not in London or Geneva but . . . in North Carolina? Who would have believed it? Secondly, this award requires $175.00 cash for an unlaminated Proclamation, which fee applies toward all crafting processes plus postage and handling to anywhere in the world. There must be a lot of work involved in slapping one of these babies together and dropping it in a mail slot. And if unlaminated is considered tacky in some quarters, a laminated Proclamation using Finland Birch wood is available at a modest cost of $250.00.

Now, there's a real bargain!

Other groups are now jumping on my bandwagon. Nearly every day the mailman delivers winning Sweepstakes entries and additional guarantees of fabulous prizes. I am looking at one this very moment in which I have successfully completed the first two stages (lucky me) and have entered the final stage toward being awarded a luxury automobile or $10,000 cash, two round-trip airfares to the Bahamas, a color television, a video camera or a $1,250 cashier's check. Who entered my name in this pot?

Somehow it seems I have finally turned my humdrum life around. No more living from paycheck to paycheck, no more pinching pennies to buy my dog a bone or my wife some new unmentionables. Easy street must be just around the corner with fame, fortune and champagne in the cooler.

With all these notable honors and fantastic financial windfalls, it's really difficult to remain the same unassuming ordinary humble great person that I've always been. I should probably give thought to writing my autobiography since they are the rage these days. All great men are writing their autobiographies and some even wind up in the cinema. It could happen to any of us and since we are all writers, we probably have an advantage over folks who would have to hire ghostwriters. If they ever made a movie of my life I would like Burt Reynolds to have the starring role. We have so much in common, he and I. Square jaw, blue eyes, sense of humor. Yep! Burt Reynolds would be perfect.

Clint Eastwood would be second choice. Men of few words, that's us. "Go ahead punk! Make my day!" I have often said those very words. And why shouldn't they make a film about me? Look at the every day, ordinary, typically average, handsome, courageous, deserving people of whom movies are written. I certainly fall in there somewhere. The only question is; which actor best exemplifies my personal attributes?

A talent search might be appropriate. It could be expanded to include all sections of the country, except New York of course. That would seem to rule out Sylvester Stallone and Al Pacino, both capable actors but neither one possessing that special charm so inherent in gentleman from the South. I mean, you either have it or you don't.

Burt and Clint and me, we have it.

I could direct the film myself and also write the script. It would begin with my birth on that fateful day in May during the Great Depression. My father, Colonel Beauregard Lynn, is pacing the floor in our nine bedroom log cabin, smoking cigars and sipping mint juleps while my mother, beautiful and vivacious as ever, is attended to by the best physicians in Atlanta.

The blessed event comes quickly because southern women are not allowed to endure prolonged suffering. Primarily though because I am in a tremendous hurry to get here. I can't wait to start carving my own path, to fulfill my destiny and to promote life, liberty and the American way.

It should be obvious why Burt and Clint have the edge here.

My childhood moves with painstaking care through the usual stages ⎯ the national marbles championship, the Eagle Scout ceremony, my no-hitter at Williamsport, and my first romance. Helen Henderson (little Brooke Shields) and I fall in love and make a vow that someday we will marry (naturally, following her successful stage career and my election to the Presidency).

The events are slightly blurred after that but I'd fill in the holes as we went along with modest but nonetheless heroic wartime exploits, financial triumphs, and the Pulitzer Prize for literature. It would be an effort to restrict the film to three hours duration but even "A Fist Full Of Dollars" can approach tedium if too lengthy.

In real life, my wife (who is not Helen Henderson or Brooke Shields) frankly offers little support toward the possibility of a movie based on my life and even pooh-poohs Burt or Clint in the likely starring role. She points out that I am neither Ghandi nor Indiana Jones and if a movie was made about me it would undoubtedly cast Wally Cox as my younger self and Mickey Rooney as I am now.

I am grieved by her attitude.

Hopefully, neither Burt nor Clint will ever hear about this.

CHAPTER TWENTY-SIX

We Americans expect our leaders of commerce and government to be dynamic and technically skilled individuals because of their high-level positions. After all, the aim of big business is to make money, lots of money, and the purpose of government is to provide for the well being of all citizens. These are serious matters and as such should be in the hands of serious, sober-minded leaders. Strong hands directed by educated professionals and highly trained bureaucrats, unbiased and competent. These are unquestionable qualities essential for leadership in all great nations. Critical issues are routinely entrusted to these corporate and civil service managers that have an impact upon us all.

So just how serious and sober-minded are they? Do they lead and do they rule with an impassive iron hand? If so, is there no levity whatever at the top? Some critics contend that the established corporate and government world is frightened of a possible outbreak of original humor at the employee level. They contend that the existence of comedic wit among subordinates or clients might tend to detract from technical and financial affairs. Consequently, the presence of humor at committee meetings and behind closed office doors is discouraged and bosses are thus classified as "grumpy pusses."

The upshot of this situation is that many executive positions are occupied by persons without a sense of humor who fail to recognize their own unintentional but amusing offerings. Anne

Denton, executive secretary for a large multinational firm in Marietta, Georgia, often witnessed telephone conversations and official correspondence in which company executives displayed faulty but entertaining vocabularies.

"Between their verbal gaffes and written faux pas," she advised, "I could write a book." Well, Miss Denton never got around to writing that book but she did share some of her laughable observations.

"He's in a tinnious situation!" said one executive.

"I like the president he's setting", said another and the rest just seemed to overflow with ease.

"He's going to hell in a handbag."

"I can speak from where I'm coming from."

"I have been made abreast of this."

"After a while, my mind starts to run together."

"There's been a lot of water under the dam."

"This will cullimate in a sale."

"People seem to percipitate around what they are most comfortable."

"It will be nice to meet you. You've been just a disemboweled voice."

Such tidbits may serve as evidence that the dynamic, technically skilled, high-level manager may not be quite as erudite as he believes himself to be. It may be amusing but also somewhat tragic that humor is being made at his expense. He has no problem in conversing orally with other dynamic people, possibly because they speak the same misconceived language.

The other side of the corporate coin presents a conflicting view, which holds that humor effectively combats job stress and tension, improves communication, raises productivity and also increase profits. In many instances employees are encouraged to display comic strips on bulletin boards and to exchange gag gifts as methods of establishing a favorable work environment.

Dr. Evelyn E. White, Ph.D., a psychologist with a lucrative practice in Columbus, Ohio, points out that humor can be an efficient management tool. "Whimsical stories or amusing jokes shared with fellow workers often go a long way toward resolving problems by easing tension and bringing employees closer together." Dr. White goes on to say that any business firm or government agency that looks upon humor as essential to an employee's attitude is a good place to work.

So, you bosses out there take note. Laugh and your corporate world laughs with you. You'll feel better for it, your staff and work groups will enjoy what they're doing, the Dow Jones may reflect a positive change and perhaps no one will call you grumpy pusses anymore. All this really doesn't have much to do with writers but it could apply to publishers and their editorial staff. Writers, artists, musicians, business leaders — they are all craftsmen in their own right and each has a beginning point.

Dr. White also suggested music as a corporate tool to increase production through the uplifting attitude of happy employees. I once spent my entire monthly allowance of two dollars on a Marine Bank harmonica. That two bucks would have taken me to eight Saturday movie serials or one bleacher seat at Sportsman's Park to watch the Browns. During the following months I practiced religiously on the chromatic scale until I was able to play "Oh Susanna" and "Old Folks At Home" without a clinker. I loved that harmonica. I practiced even in bed at night while hiding under the covers to mute the sound.

Luther Adler was my hero at that time. A virtuoso of the mouth organ, Adler played several instruments of different sizes and in different keys with half notes and he alternated back and forth in rapid succession while fluttering his hands for a tremolo effect. I would have given another month's allowance to be able to trill and flute the notes as he did.

But it was not to be. I never progressed beyond "Oh Susanna." I later tried to play the guitar but my talent was just not equal to the desire. I couldn't manage the accordion with its keyboard and bellows configuration. The banjo sounded too tinny, horns were very loud and ukuleles much too collegiate. My chin was the problem where fiddles were concerned. A strong chin was a definite requirement, all right. Not only that but fiddles were easily confused with violins and good ole boys from Georgia naturally resented any misguided soul who dared call a fiddle, a violin. Somehow I never discovered the right instrument for me to play.

Nothing seemed to work. I would never, never be a musician. The whole idea had begun innocently with that first harmonica. Such a harmless little thing it was but despite my desperate yearning, I was never the artiste I dreamed of being. Still, I can admire a shiny new Hohner mouth organ biding its lonesome time in a music store window, waiting for someone to come along and rescue it.

Perhaps someone like me.

CHAPTER TWENTY-SEVEN

People who consider themselves to be trendsetters and up-to-date, pride themselves on keeping current with all that happens in the world around them. They subscribe to morning and afternoon newspapers and watch CNN regularly to be certain they are not missing out on important events. Yet there comes a time when someone mentions a happening for which few are aware and guilt then begins to gnaw away at them for carelessly allowing such an insidious oversight to take place.

Any writer worth half his salt will assume the responsibility of filling in those instances which somehow fall through the crack of time; those little known occurrences that for one reason or another fails to register with folks as they should have.

For instance, how many folks are aware than on Tuesday, November 2, 1993, Absolutely Nobody died in Oakland, California. Now ordinarily that would be something worth celebrating but not in this case because Absolutely Nobody was the name of an actual person. The obituary said he was thirty-seven and that he legally changed his name from David Powers during an unsuccessful bid for the office of Lieutenant Governor of the State of Washington. Mr. Nobody's campaign slogan was, "Hi. I'm Absolutely Nobody. Vote for me."

You see, that was a fact for which not everyone was knowledgeable. We could go back further in time to the year 1893 when Bill Nye, a member of the World Future Society offered this sage prediction. "Women will never want the right of suffrage.

There will not be enough of them who want it," he said, "to ever encourage the menfolks to give it to them." Poor old Bill is probably still gyrating in his grave.

Does the name Robert Wadlow ring a bell? He was born in 1918 at Alton, Illinois and became a local celebrity because of his extraordinary size resulting from an overactive pituitary gland. At age eleven he wore a size twenty-five shoe and eventually achieved a height of 8 feet 11.1 inches and a weight of 439 pounds. Before his death in 1940, Robert Wadlow liked to watch midget auto races and he was often seen at a race track in south St. Louis. A friendly man, Mr. Wadlow always smiled at the children who crowded around him wherever he went. He waved to all who greeted him while peering over the grandstands to watch the cars zoom along the track.

This same race concourse also saw Pepper Martin and Dizzy Dean of the old St. Louis Cardinals baseball team. They too liked the midget cars so much that they would occasionally don helmets and squeeze their large bodies into the small vehicles to take a lap or two around the track. Fans were often delighted but not surprised to hear the voices of this duo booming over the loudspeaker system as they announced a race from the broadcast booth.

Is there anyone who knows about the Green family cemetery located at the highest point of a mountain in Pleasant Shade, Tennessee? Descendants are fond of recalling that the first family member to be interred there chose that particular site because, "It'll be the closest I'll ever get to heaven."

Let us not forget the Katz family in rural Missouri. There was Mrs. Katz and the twins Bobby and Dale. The family itself was not particularly remarkable except for Mr. Katz. He was the county dogcatcher.

Police in Fargo, North Dakota, recently reported that someone stole a car but became stuck in a quagmire of mud and water. They stole another car and tried again to pass through the same location but suffered the same result. Once more the thief stole a pickup truck and traveled along the same road only to become mired at the same place. All three vehicles were discovered the next morning, unscathed but firmly bogged down in the mud. The perpetrator was neither located nor identified.

Patients treated at a hospital in Tucker, Georgia, can personally testify that the surgical staff once included doctors with the unlikely names of Haight, Payne, Schook, Tremble and Burymann.

Speaking of hospitals, an operating room brawl in Worcester, Massachusetts, involved a surgeon and his anesthesiologist who scuffled briefly on the sanitized floor. They soon called a truce and resumed the operation while their anesthetized elderly female patient slept soundly nearby. Hospital authorities declined to discuss the matter but unofficial sources revealed that the surgeon was preparing to begin surgery when his assistant suddenly swore at him. This caused the surgeon to pick up a cotton-tipped prep stick, which he threw at the other and the fight was on. It was not noted whether the combatants re-scrubbed before continuing with their work or if the patient suffered vague recollections of being at ringside during a wrestling bout.

A man was arrested in Indianapolis after he fired six bullets into his television set because his 41-channel cable TV service provided him with *nothing* to watch. In his defense he complained, "I don't see why a man can't shoot his own TV if he wants to."

Other writers should note that stories are out there if you take the time to look for them. Time is the universal lament of all artists. There is never enough of it for it hastens in its flight on fancy wings of a poet's dream.

> Where does it go,
> Why does it haunt us so?
> Of all our precious treasures,
> Time is the least we know.

We all decry its passing for the opportunities lost, things we might have done, loves we could have known. Little thought was given to whatever time we did have for the singing of a song, the writing of a poem, the painting of a portrait. It is unfortunate but we tend to forget that, unlike us, time is immortal and can therefore set its own pace while we mourn for tasks unfinished. Tasks that somehow become mere memories.

Memories incidentally are one of the most important attributes in a writer's inventory. Much of the material that finds its way into print began as a memory. There is a virtual fount of knowledge lying just beneath the surface of our consciousness. It feeds our unspoken plea for first-hand information during our never-ending research on writing projects. The many reference sources employed by writers are very good, in fact they're great, but our own memories comprise the best resource we have. Memories and imagination together form a strength of unity that writers cannot exist without. Let me cite the following example.

A young man, browsing through antiquated books and discolored magazines at a book store in Atlanta, discovered an original copy of "Mystery Incarnate," a local author's celebrated narrative poem and one of the rarest of American books.

"I was first skeptical and then amazed," said William J. Bergman, "to see it lying there in plain view on a pile of assorted pamphlets, apparently overlooked because of its nondescript appearance."

Bergman paid $25 for the 28-page volume, which has since been valued by Sotheby's New York auction house at nearly a half-million dollars. Only seven copies of this particular book are known to exist today. The book is considered a priceless gem in any collection because it was the author's first acclaimed work and is notably scarce. According to Clint Richards, proprietor of Buckhead Books and Manuscripts, this original copy was obtained by him at a wholesale auction last year and has been lying unnoticed since then on a table containing miscellaneous publications.

"It is a true piece of Americana," said its purchaser who is an avid collector of rare books. "I realized it was a bargain purchase but never dreamed it was worth as much as half a million dollars."

Mystery Incarnate is an epic poem relating the adventure of a young lady in a mythological world in which she defends her mirrored image, accused of murder. It was published when the author was residing in Lawrenceville, a suburb of Atlanta.

Modesty prevents me from divulging the identity of that poet or the seed of imagination that spawned the article itself.

CHAPTER TWENTY-EIGHT

The times which are a-comin' will be blessed with profuse pearls of poetry offered by contemporary writers, many of whom are yet unrecognized. They are yet as little known as I am and I consider myself indeed fortunate to have exchanged pleasantries with some of them. Their work may ascend to that poetic pinnacle which often arrives, sad to say, after the breath of life departs.

So, in this small space, let me recount those with whom I have crossed paths long enough to say, "Howdy!"

There was Judson Jerome of Writers Digest. I met him at Ocala, Florida, during a writer's conference in 1986. At the same time I met Florence Bradley, editor of Editor's Desk, Robert Newton Peck, author of the "Soup And Me" series, Jo Anne Heckler and Janet Konkle, poets and writers all.

My correspondents have included Mary Sewall Hebert, Kay Bunt, and Charlotte Deskins from our Round Robin Club, Clay Harrison, George Koch, and Sharon Harris plus Patricia Ide, Marian Ford Park, Rosa Nelle Anderson, Angie Monnens, Mavis Harrell, Mildred Keel and Esther Leiper. Esther is actually Esther Estabrooks, poetry editor of Writer's Journal. There is Linda Hutton, editor and publisher of Rhyme Time and Mystery Time; Charlie Fabrizio, editor of Z Miscellaneous; Denver Stull, editor and publisher of Parnassus Literary Journal; Tom Bergeron of Anterior Publications; Bill Halbert of Sharing & Caring; and writers Kay Harvey, Janice Power and Mary Webster Griffin.

There are others that I admire for their individual work but whom I have not met or corresponded with such as Howard Nemerov, Robert Creeley, Alice Mackenzie Swaim, William Stafford, Louis Simpson, and John Ashberry. Talented all, yet how many names mentioned here will be familiar one hundred years from now?

I also number among my correspondents a certain gentleman who resides at the North Pole. Yes, it's Santa Claus and I used to write him more often than in recent years. As a matter of fact, my most recent letter was right after last Christmas. I kinda got upset with him and took the occasion to blow off a little steam. I don't mind sharing that letter even with the risk that he might not visit my house during the coming holiday season.

"Dear Santa," the letter began. "I know it's late to be writing because Christmas has indeed come and gone and you're probably still resting up after your busy trip to the four corners of the earth. No doubt you're exhausted from your travels and from passing out presents and goodies to all the good little boys and girls. But that's what I want to talk to you about.

"In past years you visited regularly at Christmas and for that I am certainly grateful. I have fond memories of the tingly anticipation as each day brought your scheduled arrival a little closer, and the dreams of wonderful toys you would leave for me. I was always among the good little boys and girls and I hung my stocking by the chimney with care hoping that soon you would be there. On that great night I nestled snug in my bed with visions of sugar plums dancing in my head, waiting for the sound of such clatter that made me leap from my bed to see what was the matter. Each time I saw by the light of the moon reflecting off newly fallen snow, a miniature sleigh and eight tiny reindeer.

"So you see, Santa, I'm not some recent convert to the fact of your existence. I've believed in you all my life. That's why I find it difficult to understand why you still bring me little cars and trucks and tin soldiers and cowboy hats and baseball gloves and sweaters and stuff like that. I'm still the same good little boy I've always been, but Santa, I'm more than sixty years old now and it would've been nice to get something different this Christmas.

"Oh, I still feel that tingly anticipation of your coming visit and my dreams are yet filled with wonderful things I hope you would bring. However, I've outgrown the little cars and trucks of bygone years. I'm a writer now, Santa, and I've been sort of hoping for, well, a new computer keyboard for one thing. My old one lost two key caps and the space bar sticks once in a while. Then, there was the time I accidentally spilled coffee on it. It would have been nice if you had brought me some extra floppy disks or even some ribbon cartridges for my printer.

"There's lots of other neat gift ideas for writers, Santa. Desk lamps, copy holders, three-hole punchers, paper trimmers, print wheels, note pads, postage stamps. The list is endless so there's really no reason to continue bringing those cowboy hats and sweaters.

"I really hate to bother you when you've probably got your feet propped high and a warm eggnog at hand. Mrs. Claus is surely glad to have you home again and your elves are most likely cavorting gaily in the snow while giving no thought to next year's production. Perhaps Rudolph is getting his nose recharged. Still, I think it's important to bring to your attention before you make your plans for next year that my needs have changed.

"It's a different world we live in, Santa, and unlike you, we don't all remain the same age forever. I know you think of me as that good little fellow who obeys his mother and father and never causes trouble, but please don't bring me any little cars and trucks next Christmas. If you insist on bringing any toys at all, a new Pentium 166mhz computer with CD-ROM and a FAX-Modem would be nice and I could certainly use a laser-jet color printer.

"For now though, just lean back and relax in your favorite easy chair. Take it easy and think of the happiness you have brought to the good little boys and girls this year. Imagine how much more joy you could bring to those of us who happen to be somewhat older and have different gift wishes.

"Every day from now until next Christmas will be filled with tingly anticipation. It will be especially so on that night before when all through my house not a creature will stir, not even a mouse. I'll hang my stocking by the chimney with care and dream of hi-tech playthings and fancy software until I soon hear on the roof the prancing and pawing of each little hoof. Down the chimney you'll come with a bound, dressed in fur from head to foot and your clothes will be covered with ashes and soot. I'll watch from my hiding place as you unwrap your pack and deposit the goodies from IBM or Mac.

"A word to the wise is what I always say and that's why I'm waiting for next Christmas day. Oh, I'll play with those little cars and trucks and tin soldiers and cowboy hats because I really do like them but please don't forget that this little boy is a grown-up boy now Santa, and I still believe in you."

CHAPTER TWENTY-NINE

This is Roland Harrington of the Public Broadcasting System speaking from the Peachtree Street Book Store in another of a series of documentaries on the literary appetites of casual book browsers.

Here comes a browser now.

Good afternoon sir. I'm conducting a survey on the reading habits of the American public and I would like to ask you a few questions.

Sure thing, son. Fire away.

OK. First of all, what is your name?

C.J. Harper. My name's really Charles Jerome Harper but folks always call me C.J. I'm from Loganville.

Fine. Now, Mr. Harper . . .

C.J., son. Call me C.J. I don't answer to nothing else.

Very well, uh, C.J. Tell me. What kind of books do you read?

I don't have time to read books son. Too many words in 'em. Long words, fancy words, foreign words. Don't have time to wade through a lot of fancy foreign words. No sir. I do enjoy this book though.

You mean that book under your arm?

Yep.

What's the title of it?

It don't have a title. In fact, it don't have nothing. No pictures. No long words, No foreign words. My kind of book, son.

But, uh, C.J., all the pages are blank.

That's right, son. Nothing on 'em to clutter my mind.

Well, that could be a selling point, I suppose, but isn't it unusual to read a book that don't have any writing?

I didn't say I was reading this book, son. I said that I enjoy it.

Can you explain?

Sure thing. You see, I'm a writer and . . .

What! You're a writer and you don't read books with words in them?

Let me finish.

Sorry.

Most writers read books by other writers and then try to write something original. But somehow they always seem to include in their own writings a few words or phrases literally borrowed from other writers. You follow what I'm saying?

I'm not sure.

Plagiarism, son. Pure and simple. Oh, they don't mean to do it. It's just something that can't be helped. You read a good book and it stays with you while you're plotting and characterizing and dialoguing. Before you know it, you've taken someone else's story — lock, stock and protagonist. That's why I never read other writer's books.

But that doesn't explain why you carry a book with blank pages.

It's plain enough, son. Books are the symbols of a writer's profession. I carry a book to let everyone know that I'm a writer and the pages are blank to prevent my accidental borrowing of another writer's words.

How many books have you written?

Well actually, none yet but I'm working on a volume of poetry at the moment and I expect it to be a best seller.

Don't tell me . . .

Yep. It's a book of blank verse.

This is Roland Harrington, Public Broadcasting System, with another stirring interview at the crossroads of time.

When the ashes of time are sufficiently stirred, strange notions are aroused. Now it seems that certain foreign interests recently proposed that Wilbur and Orville Wright were not the first to fly an airplane. Is nothing truly sacred anymore? Must we continue to suffer intrusions and defamations of our national values simply because of our American heritage?

Repercussions had not yet subsided in the furor over the Wright brothers when one of our own countrymen, a descendant of Betsy Ross, stepped forth to deny that his famous forefather, or foremother in this case, wielded any influence in the design of the American flag. "Oh, she may have sewn some kind of banner," he said. "After all, she did live in Philadelphia at the time."

Not to be surpassed in assaults upon American treasures, the National Geographic Society now reports that Christopher Columbus first landed in the new world on a small insignificant island known as Samana Cay and not at San Salvador as history records it.

A prudent person might seriously consider the plausibility of other assertions of careless facts currently being imparted to our children in classrooms throughout the nation. What are they to believe? Or, as one skeptical Clemson Freshman was recently heard to remark, "Hey man! If a dude can't trust his history book, who can he trust?"

What if these are not isolated instances? Suppose a conspiracy exists to keep us from learning terrible secrets of our past. Would we still be able to hold our heads high if we perhaps discovered that Ben Franklin never owned a kite, or a dime store? How would we feel to learn that Millard Fillmore was a figment of someone's imagination?

We may yet hope for the perpetuation of other revered heroes and institutions. At the least we may be secure in the poetry of Robert Frost and the prose of Robert Louis Stevenson. We may be grateful that little Orphan Annie will remain at pre-puberty forever and Dolly Parton did not.

In recapping the secrets being divulged intentionally or prematurely, one has only to recall the words of Richard Nixon who reportedly commented, "It could have been worse."

CHAPTER THIRTY

There is some disagreement among writers concerning personal computers and just how user friendly they are. Well, how friendly *can* they be and how friendly do we want them to be? I have a PC and I can't really boast about the love and affection I get from it.

In my opinion, computers are not as friendly as my GMC pickup and that truck has stood by me through hail, rain, sleet, and late payments and has never complained. Oh, once it kept repeating "pucketa, pucketa, pucketa" but that was my fault and the pucketas disappeared whenever I added three quarts of 10W40.

I've heard some say that their PC purrs like a kitten. Maybe so but that doesn't prove they're friendly. Cats purr all the time and they aren't the least bit friendly. I've never seen a cat run in circles and wag its tail when its master comes home from a hard day at the office. If anything, cats are barely tolerant of the hand that feeds them. The same thing can be said about a computer. They are barely tolerant of the hand that strokes their keyboard and very unforgiving if that hand accidentally deletes a file instead of saving it. There is no "oops" key to call upon and that cursor continues to blink off-on, off-on, as if to say, "Hey look everybody! My human just made a boo-boo."

Many different kinds of PCs are now in use. Their micro chips are either old or new, their speeds vary to 166MHz and beyond, their RAMs and hard drives are counted in gigabytes and response times are measured in nano seconds. It doesn't matter! They're all alike.

Barely tolerant.

They know they're smarter than flesh and blood and they delight in sending embarrassing little messages across their screens to show us up.

ERROR! ERROR! YOUR CONFIGURATION IS INCORRECT! PLEASE BEGIN AGAIN! This usually happens when a co-worker or a 10-year old neighbor's child is present to snicker and to repeat the message loud enough for everybody else to hear.

Computer users must attend school to learn how to turn on their PC and to run the various software programs. By contrast, all a computer has to do is digest the installed program and it's ready to go. Strangely enough, software programs do not work on all computers and it is the responsibility of the user to determine which programs are compatible with his particular PC. Don't ask the PC. It won't say anything until you try it and if it doesn't work then, you get a snide message. DISK READ ERROR! PLEASE CANCEL, ABORT, OR RETRY! You can't hear it but your PC is laughing up its electronic sleeve. "Hey look everybody! My human just made another boo-boo."

If it was really user friendly, it would have downplayed the whole unfortunate incident and maybe offered suggestions on what to do next instead of leaving you out there to be ridiculed. There's always some traitorous human nearby who has attended more microcomputer study groups or who has more experience, one who relishes pointing out your electronic shortcomings. Your PC could save you from all this if it was really user friendly.

Computers are no longer a luxury of the future. We have now moved into that future and PCs are today's necessity. The typewriter we used in the old days belongs in museums alongside Stone Age clubs and Model T Fords. They have not only been replaced by computers, they have become symbolic of old fogeys who are unable to adapt to the changing times. If you still own a typewriter, hide it in the closet or in the attic before it marks you as an old fogey.

Although the usual input device for a computer is the keyboard, it is not absolutely necessary for the user to be a typist. There are special function keys on the keyboard that are used in word processing and in manipulating various programs. A mouse is another input device that controls the cursor on the screen. All of these gadgets are there for the purpose of providing the user with the mistaken belief of being in command. The PC normally goes along with everything the user asks except for a few instances in which it decides to exercise its independence. It then develops a glitch, for which no amount of coddling or threats will resolve until the PC tires of its own little game and gives in.

This is not being user friendly.

In fact, beginners would be wise to consider their forthcoming experience with computers as not unlike stepping into a battle zone. The relationship will not be a friendly one. Danger lurks everywhere, in every byte, behind each attribute. Every time you boot it up you will wonder just what will go wrong this time but don't expect your PC to give you a motherly pat on the head or even a good word. Its vocabulary, while not limitless, is dedicated to speaking in unknown tongues and you will not understand what's happening unless you are well versed in computerese and have developed a thick skin.

PCs do what they want to do when they want to do it and are friendly enough as long as their humans understand the roles that each are assigned. Otherwise, it will blink its cursor accusingly and proclaim, "Hey world! My human just made another stupid boo-boo."

CHAPTER THIRTY-ONE

During my sophomore English class at Herky High, I learned that a writer was only as good as the tools with which he surrounds himself. "Those tools," Miss Higgins explained, "are a writer's knowledge of spelling and grammar."

I had no great problem with spelling but the subtle arrangement of words into phrases and the punctuation of sentences was entirely another matter. I could manipulate multi-syllabic words with comparative ease. However, I could not cope with commas, semicolons, exclamation points, or two-em dashes. It had become my habit to insert either a comma or semicolon within lengthy sentences whenever my writing needed to pause for breath; sort of like separating the cars of a runaway freight train. If my words were particularly exciting I would call for an exclamation point after the caboose. I never did learn the difference between a one-em and a two-em dash.

I fully understood there was a direct relationship between visual written language and oral patterns of speech. What gave me the most trouble was the use of participial phrases. Because of their position within a sentence they occasionally falsely modified or related to a word in a humorous or otherwise preposterous manner. Miss Higgins, who normally was a sweet and sensitive teacher, nevertheless delighted in sharing aloud with my classmates, such gems of mine as, "Being full of curves, she had trouble keeping her car on the road."

Professional writers are extremely careful in their use of

participial modifiers to avoid being unintentionally amusing or patently absurd. But even if they escape such embarrassments, writers may yet confuse a reader by positioning a verbal phrase so close to its subjective word that logic is momentarily suspended. In that case, the phrase is said to "dangle." I recall a letter once written by a favorite aunt in which she expressed concern for her little dog. She wrote, "Running through the orchard and foaming at the mouth, I was greatly worried about Skippy." We were more worried about Aunt Erma. It was good for a family laugh but I have since fallen into that same snare more than once.

Participial perils have pursued me relentlessly in my writing career and on page 124 of my unpublished mystery novel "Hung Jury," I described a police investigation thus: "Continuing to search the victim's bedroom for evidence, the revolver eluded detection." A few pages later I wrote, "Losing control, Agnes crashed through the barricade and veered across the median, damaging her front end extensively."

Incorrect placement of participial phrases is an easy trap for careless writers. It is especially so during wee morning hours when writers are quite vulnerable to mental lapses while laboring to meet a deadline or when the wife announces that her pains are two minutes apart.

A recent essay on participial perils generated an inquiry from Joan Barton, editor of Detective Cryptograms. "I would love to have you write a story for publication that is full of those crazy mixed up sentences," she said. Her proposal sounded interesting so I quickly busied myself with an adventure story that eventually numbered 3,200 words. I titled it, "The Golden Buddha Of Pashiwar." Ms. Barton later advised that she was interested in something less than 800 words. She also furnished two sample copies of her publication and I realized we were on two separate wave lengths. Her stories were told in numbered sentences and encrypted into code letters; therefore, the name "Cryptogram." What was I to do with my 3,200-word mystery?

I became intrigued after a day or two of introspection and inasmuch as this editor went to the trouble of soliciting something from me for publication, I decided to give it a try after all.

My previous story became, "The Case Of The Stolen Whatzis," and was reduced to about 900 words in fifty-seven numbered sentences. I had intended to excerpt selected parts of the original tale, which I did. However, it was necessary to change the ending for brevity. The result: I now had two mystery adventures ⁻ one short, one long. This editor was pleased with the short story and the longer version was mailed off to another publication. There's no particular moral to this narrative, just a lesson learned!

More than a few years have passed since my high school English Lit days and I have finally reached a compromise with commas, semicolons, and exclamation points. I still do not understand two-em dashes nor is my novel yet published, although I am certain that it will someday be a bestseller, unless those dangling demons have the last laugh after all.

Often when acquaintances learn for the first time that I am a published poet they invariably ask, "What kind of poems do you write?" Privately I had to admit to myself that I really don't know how to respond to this question so a layman would understand. My responses aloud vary according to my own interpretation (right or wrong) of the questioner's sincere interest. Is he merely making polite conversation or does he actually want to know? I have heard myself utter inane comments like; "Oh I write fun poetry," or even, "You know, the usual stuff. I write long ones and I write short ones."

I have yet to answer that question to my personal satisfaction and feel compelled to give flip responses because I am suspicious of the genuine interest behind such a question. Am I being asked if I write in rhyme or free verse, lyric or satire, narrative or dramatic? Is the inquirer wanting to know whether I write nice little rhyming verses or poems with unusual words requiring a dictionary? It is fairly certain that a poet would not ask such a question of another poet. Yet, because this is a common question asked by those who must have read some poetry in their lifetime, it should not be considered frivolous but deserving of a serious reply. Therefore, I have asked myself — well, what kind of poetry do I write?

For all its absolute sincerity, the question is no easier to answer. I am aware of my own reading preferences and that I lean toward poetry that possesses a definite rhythm or meter, beauty and grace, and with a most important characteristic that makes me feel as if the poem was created just for me. I enjoy lyrical poetry and narrative poems with story lines, humorous situations, and patriotic themes. Conversely, I dislike that which is non-metrical in structure, pretentious in language, and vague in poetic purpose.

It seems reasonable then that I would write the kind of poetry that I enjoy reading myself. However, it doesn't work quite that way. The truth is, when I sit at my keyboard I have only the barest thread of an idea and no matter how I consciously attempt to guide my creative thoughts in a particular direction, my muse takes over and the poem proceeds towards its individual goal. My contribution may not even be recognized throughout the poem. True, I do the actual writing or typing but an initial idea often develops words in an opening line then gathers other words for support and the poem begins. In this manner, the flow of thought continues. Stanzas or other natural divisions are revised and polished until the poem reaches an obvious ending. The final product may have assumed an entirely different identity in format, style, and content than originally intended. This is how a poem grows and progresses with very little assistance or interruption from the poet.

Subsequent poems are created in a similar manner but are yet unlike in their composition and impact. This being the case, how then can I answer the question as to the kind of poetry that I write? I have absolutely no idea of my writing mood from one moment to the next and mood is the catalyst behind all poets.

Perhaps the question itself as originally posed is faulty. Maybe it should be amended to ask — what kind of poetry have you written?

A quick review of the several hundred poems in my personal library discloses quatrains, sestets, septets, octaves, epic poems presenting views of nature, love, death, mythology, religion, and the resolution of all problems involving mankind. Some poems rhyme while others do not. Some are good, some are not, some are published while most are not, but they all have one commonality. They are each different. There is no recurring theme or pattern except they sound good when read aloud and they have gifted me with a real sense of self-satisfaction as I read them over again.

What kind of poet am I? Well, I enjoy poems written by others and I thrill at knowing someone else may be reading one of my own little verses at any magical moment. I am a poet who sees poetry everywhere I look.

What kind of poems do I write? Oh, I write long ones and I write short ones.

CHAPTER THIRTY-TWO

When the French impressionist Pierre Bonnard died in 1947, his creations had already been exhibited in the Louvre and other major museums throughout Europe. He was recognized by the world of art as a legend in his own time. Yet, he was not satisfied with anything he had done.

"Papa" Bonnard was a perfectionist.

Often during a museum visit, he would decide that one of his paintings was not exactly as he liked and would proceed to improve it on the spot to the consternation of curators. It was explained to him that the national treasures of France were not to be tampered with, not even by their own creator.

While it is admirable to be eternally striving for idealism it is equally important to know when to cry, "Halt! — Enough!" There comes a moment when the literary offspring must be shunted away to stand on its own merit, and its creator to develop a closed mind to further "corrections." Never mind that there will always be someone who will complain how it should have been done, for critics abound in the woodwork and beneath rocks and they tend to speak without saying anything.

It is especially so in this enlightened era.

Writers and poets are accustomed to editorial rejection but they are not prepared to be critiqued by quibbling arbiters, well-intentioned peers, or even family members who traditionally are the staunchest allies of struggling artists. The offering of a poem or short story for critical review is thus not unlike trying on a hangman's noose for size or voluntarily placing one's head in a guillotine. "OK, Pierre, I think it's sharp enough now!" In effect, the poet/writer is submitting his soul for an in-depth analysis whenever he allows his work to be scrutinized and judged.

Every artist is a purist who suffers from a desire for perfection but is frustrated whenever his work falls short. This seems to have been borne out by the poet Paul Valery who ascribed to the unique theory that an artist never really finishes his work; he merely abandons it.

Attaining perfection should not necessarily be confused with achieving a state of artistic excellence. However, this reality will not deter him from seeking the impossible dream, and rightfully it should not. Dreams are the basic material of success and success may truthfully be assessed by how near a person comes to the pinnacle of their dream. Consequently, while perfection may not be a realistic goal, poets and writers can appease that inner drive with the realization that, everything considered, they did pretty well!

Doing pretty well is something to be proud of due to various obstacles that intimidate and sometimes terrify the weak at heart. Even the most outspoken poets and writers have their moments of vulnerability when certain things tend to intimidate them. A few writers feel threatened because they haven't yet learned to use a computer. Others are dismayed when the telephone rings and it's never for them. I used to feel intimidated because I didn't own a pickup truck like all my neighbors. Not those big-wheel monsters that are more at home at a tractor pull or dinosaur hunt. I'm talking about a regular size pickup that can roam city streets as well as country back roads hauling 2X4s or little league ball players with equal pride.

In my hometown when a passenger car and a pickup find themselves next to each other at a traffic signal, it's the driver of the automobile who feels strangely inadequate. He steals an admiring glance at the other vehicle and wishes in his heart that he could trade places with the other driver. He may be a very successful businessman driving an expensive foreign sports model. Perhaps he owns a large home in the city and another overlooking the ocean, but if he doesn't drive a pickup truck it's difficult for him to hold his head up among his fellow man.

It's a macho thing.

Cars come in different sizes and are variously equipped with all sorts of gizzies to make driving more comfortable, but regardless of how fancy they are, they're still pipsqueaks when standing next to a pickup. They just don't project that free spirit image or devil-may-care posture that comes automatically to the driver of a GMC long bed boasting a V-8 engine, twin CB antennas, a sliding rear window, aluminum guard rails and an old hound dog pacing back and forth, daring little BMWs to approach on either side.

It's not a criticism that the pickup may be old or its paint is fading and peeling. What counts is that it represents a symbol of independence and competence. The driver of such a vehicle is surely able to handle anything that comes his way regardless whether it's a flat tire, an overdue magazine article, or a flirtatious blonde perched sidesaddle on a Harley-Davidson. Whatever is needed, this is a man who can rise to the occasion.

I remember my uncle's pickup. It was a rusty 1941 Ford with running boards and a wooden bed. He worked a Missouri farm and that truck was used to haul produce as well as manure and feed and hay for the livestock. Cousin Billy and I clamored all over the hood and sides of that truck. We enjoyed many make-believe adventures yanking the steering wheel hard in simulated pursuit of bank robbers and other assorted bad guys.

My uncle talked to that old truck like a bosom pal. "Come on Lizzie," he'd say. "Let's hear you growl." Then he'd throw in the clutch, slam the floor shift lever into second for a particularly steep hill, pump the gas pedal and manhandle the choke all at the same time. Old Lizzie rattled and clanked but she climbed that hill and never seemed to mind the rough handling. Billy and I reasoned that it was important to learn how to talk to a pickup, so we practiced our truck language during our imaginary adventures.

Driving a pickup is not merely a means of transportation from one place to another. It is also a vantage point from where wider vistas are viewed. Traffic signals and pedestrians are easier to see and it's surprising to note how many people fail to wash the rooftops of their little cars. Apparently they can't see the dirt while driving so they just give it a quick wipe and let it go at that.

On the other hand, pickup owners aren't hung up on frequent wash jobs, either. The personality of a pickup truck never changes whether it's squeaky clean or sporting several months of mud and grime. When I finally did get my first pickup truck I always made it a point to wash it every Fourth of July. However, if I forgot once in a while there was no harm and my bosom pal was very understanding.

It isn't necessary to have a lot of status symbols on a pickup. If it comes with air-conditioning and automatic transmission, that's fine. If not, an AM radio that tunes in country stations is the only accessory really needed, plus an old dog to add class. The dog doesn't have to be too old and he can ride either in the back or up front. My dog, Alex, always rides next to me in the front seat. I'm sure he firmly believes that the truck actually belongs to him and that I am his personal driver. I can rely on him to wait somewhere out of sight, but when the door opens all I see is a blur as he bounds into the cab.

Dogs and pickups naturally go together. Alex prefers to take his afternoon nap lying in the cool shade underneath his truck. Staying so near gives him a good running start on any cat that might have ideas about curling up on the hood. He sits or lies contentedly on the passenger side as we drive through the country and whenever he decides that the inside air is too humid, he thrusts his head out the window to capture a cool refreshing breeze. I envy him that pleasure but I have to do the driving.

All my friends and neighbors know that I'm a down-to-earth kind of guy. I don't put on airs and I enjoy a cold beer on a hot day like anyone else. Still, I can't help but snicker just a tiny bit whenever I pull up to a traffic signal next to a passenger car. Nearly always, the other driver will slowly turn his head in my direction and I know he's wishing he could trade his whatzis for my GMC.

I don't blame him. It's only human nature to want something better than what you already have. It's the American way.

CHAPTER THIRTY-THREE

Even in this age of television, microwave ovens, and personal computers, it's a certainty that at some critical moment a power outage will occur and everything will cease to work. Darkness will descend, dogs will howl, and mothers will summon their children to bed. At that very moment, a screeching "Aaagghhh!" may be heard emanating from various corners of darkened homes giving rise to immediate suspicion that somewhere in the night a dastardly crime has just been committed. Either that or (shudder) another writer has suffered loss of word processor memory.

Computers tend to develop strange quirks that defy explanation and occasionally display undecipherable hieroglyphics on their monitors. This normally happens during quiet morning hours when future best-selling authors drag themselves from a warm comfortable bed to get an early start on the day. Glitches are commonplace then with false graphics and aborted commands sprinkled with power surges that play havoc with random access memory. Somewhere between the third cup of coffee and the first streak of dawn, line voltages appear to stabilize and machines revert to their true mechanical status. It usually coincides with floor squeaks and bathroom noises as the family rouses itself, one by one, and an author's best intentions are once more relegated to second place on life's list of priorities.

Word processing software has contributed the nodding head syndrome (NHD) to the medical world's menu of maladies. This is an affliction endured by myopic writers who must contend with bifocals during waking moments. Pity them, for theirs is the ultimate handicap of computer users. Bifocals are eyeglasses with lenses adjusted to two different focal lengths, the lower portion for focusing on nearby objects and the upper area for distant viewing. The unfortunate wearer must necessarily move his head up or down to scan either the keyboard or the monitor screen, for both cannot be simultaneously observed. The habit-forming side effects of constant positioning and repositioning of the head renders the writer easily recognizable when he ventures out in public. Laypersons may think such individuals are plagued with a nervous disorder but fellow writers are familiar with this syndrome and are quick to sympathize.

I have been burdened with NHD for several years but then last Sunday came the first visit from the kilowatt gremlin. I was already into an extended deadline on a murder mystery in which each of five prime suspects were eliminated by the brilliant logic of my amateur puzzle solver, Shamus O'Neil. The final segment was gushing smoothly onto my monitor display when the desk lamp flickered.

"Oh No!" I screamed and desperately hit the Menu Key on the Keypad. Experience taught me that it was necessary to move fast. The micro disc was activated in the module and I depressed the Return Key to hear a quiet purr signaling the transference of text to floppy disk. It was in the middle of that function when the power failed. I was enveloped in darkness, wondering whether my 50,000 words safely made the brief trip into memory storage or were forever lost in electronic space.

After my very first disaster with memory losses due to electrical storms, I adopted the habit of periodically transferring raw text to micro disc after each page. However, this was one of those occasions when I became so engrossed in Shamus O'Neil's deductive genius that I committed too much material to exposure. Forgotten in the heat of creation was that most dangerous fact of word processing; *memory is only temporary.*

Who knows how long I sat waiting, hardly daring to breathe, uttering promises to the supreme deity for His protection of my lost words and pleading for their safe return. I imagined all sorts of dire things happening to them. Were they drifting aimlessly among other homeless bytes? Did they feel abandoned, unwanted? Would I ever see them again?

Eventually the storm subsided and my computer hummed a greeting as current flowed once more through the wires and wafers feeding its hungry circuits. My fingers poised above the keyboard and gingerly recalled the word processor menu. I selected the document I had been working on and touched the command key. The familiar purring sounded once more and soon the monitor presented the option of creating, viewing, and editing. At least it didn't say, "Document Not Found." There was still hope.

With quickened heart, I pressed Edit and the screen displayed the title page of my manuscript. I scrolled to the ending and was overjoyed to learn that it was all there. Nothing had been lost after all and Shamus O'Neil was still in business.

I have since learned to combat frequent power outages with the aid of an antiquated Underwood manual typewriter and a supply of birthday candles. Now, when the lights fail I can snicker at such adversity as I align the candles for maximum visibility. A stranger might very well confuse the scene with Satanism but it works well enough to preserve ideas or certain passages that might otherwise dissipate into Never-Never Land, never to return.

There is some concern as to how He might view the candle situation and I therefore prudently add one or two entries to the list of promises made.

More than a few folks might smirk at such a trivial escapade. If so, let me caution that one of the things that aggravate an average person like me, is a smirker. I can put up with annoyances like crackers in bed and misplaced commas but a smirk really gets my Irish up. The formation of a National Association for Average People Against Smirkers (NAAPAS) doesn't sound bad at all.

Webster defines a smirker as someone who smiles in a conceited, knowing, simpering, or annoyingly complacent manner. I have met a few smirkers in my time. They are easy to recognize for their snobbish superiority and shimmering aura of self-admiration and know-it-all-ness. Fat Pat Fribley was a smirker. It wasn't enough that she was a better second baseman than me but every time she got a base hit or made a good play, Fat Pat would look in my direction and smirk.

"Stop that smirking!" I growled.

"I'm not smirking," she would say with another smirk.

"You are. You are too smirking." But someone always intervened to keep the situation under control. It was then that I developed my intense dislike for smirkers. There is something sinister and foreboding in a smirk. It may even be un-American.

Throughout history, many smirkers were notoriously offensive in their display of pompous arrogance. Mona Lisa comes readily to mind. One of the most insufferable smirkers of all time, however, has to be the inventor of those little plastic thingamajigs found in apparel stores. You know, they're those little price tag fasteners that cannot be removed without a bolo knife or blow torch. Shopping for a new pair of mittens bonded with plastic thingamajigs is thus not dissimilar to being fitted for handcuffs. Is there anyone who does not bear the scars or wounds incurred during a skirmish with those little devils?

We average people fall somewhat shy of perfection and we need all the self-confidence we can muster just to muddle through from one day to the next. The one thing we don't need is a smirker at each hurdle to remind us that we are just average people. If NAAPAS chapters were organized throughout this nation, I am certain that membership would soon exceed the combined rolls of the AFL/CIO, the VFW, and AARP. And if it so happens that the smirkers should unite with the scoffers to form a dreaded SS, it may then become necessary for the NAAPAS to go underground.

CHAPTER THIRTY-FOUR

Vacations are kind of a reward thing. People work hard all year, pay their bills, go to church on Sunday and then take a couple of weeks off to do whatever they want with no obligations and no questions asked. No fuss, just pack the car and head out.

Not so with folks dedicated to words and phrases.

First of all, writers do other things besides write. They work hard, pay their bills, go to church on Sunday and try to steal a few hours each day to write their little verses or another chapter on their novel. Their time is usually early in the morning when sleeping spouses and children are still innocently dreaming. That's the quiet time before the first rays of sunshine gently nudge nesting birds into song and a writer can collect his thoughts without distraction.

An ideal vacation for a writer is two weeks alone with only pen or keyboard for company. Bundle the family off to some exotic place. The writer will stay at home, thank you.

"But dear," says an anxious wife, "are you sure you'll be all right here by yourself?"

"Of course I will, honey. Just go on up to Ohio and enjoy yourself and don't worry about me."

"My sister Agnes could look in on you."

"I don't want your sister Agnes looking in on me."

"Suppose you get hungry."

"I know where the can opener is and I can always find a McDonald's if I run out of pork and beans."

"Well, if you're sure you'll be OK."

"I'm sure."

Loved ones frequently find it difficult to understand the need for a writer to commune with himself (or herself as the case may be). To rattle around in an empty house at any hour of the day or night is a real treat and to sit before a keyboard while engrossed in a developing story plot, sometimes barefoot or in pajamas, can be sheer ecstasy; especially if a protagonist is able to work out of a knotty tangle and THE END appears ultimately and appropriately, at the end.

Striding to the imaginary podium to receive his imaginary award, our writer will offer the usual thanks to his agent and publisher for their confidence and professional guidance, but mostly to his family for their vacation in Ohio. Yet what happens when vacation rolls around again and our writer does not have an ongoing project, no manuscript in progress, no publication deadline and no creative thought buzzing around in his head? There's no way out. He must accompany the wife and kiddies to some exotic place for an entire two weeks away from the house and out of touch with his editors and publishers.

'You'll love it dear," she says. "You can swim or fish or just lie in the sun and relax."

"Suppose I don't want to swim or fish or lie in the sun and relax?"

"Now, now. Don't be a grouch. It'll be good for you." And with that spousal edict pronounced, our hero realizes he has no choice in the matter. It's off to the beach for two weeks in the sun. Swimming, fishing, relaxing.

"Not if I can help it," he grouches. Old habits and routines are not easily abandoned so while the family packs suitcases with tanning oils and inflatable toys, he gathers his IBM laptop, the latest Writer's Digest and a pair of U.S. Air Force Rayban reflecting sunglasses. "I might have to sit in their sun," he muses, "but it'll be on my terms."

Of course there are places where writers may pursue their craft while simultaneously retaining a certain amount of privacy and seclusion. Writer colonies abound from Vermont to Key West and

California providing lodging far from the hubbub of intruding civilization. Facilities range from rustic log cabins to cabanas and up-to-date lodge retreats amid serene surroundings complete with luxurious amenities. Unfortunately there is a certain amount of suspicion on the part of some wives at the prospect of their writer husband residing in solitude for an entire week or more, unchaperoned.

"I'm not sure it's a good idea," she will say. "I've heard about those kinds of places." The news sure got around fast about that Ocala conference. But now, this is where our writer must keep a low profile and assume the attitude that he really doesn't relish the idea of spending all those days as a hermit; that it's actually more of a duty than pleasure and he would be going only because it might benefit his writing career and enhance his literary reputation.

I don't know. She might buy it. If not, there's always the beach — swimming, fishing, relaxing.

We writers have other bothersome things to contend with. It's one thing to work our brains down to the nub with finding the exact word for our little verses and stories, but we also have to contend with attacks of dry mouth and trembly knees. These things normally manifest themselves at the precise instant of discovering that intended victims are expected to give a speech before the PTA or read a poem at the National Poetry Conference. I am referring to sudden panic attacks, those pesky butterflies-in-the-tummy otherwise known as "Nervous Nellies." Such moments of temporary breakdowns are usually characterized by a nervous state in which the body erupts in a cold sweat, when neither leg agrees to cooperate, and a hard knot forms somewhere in the throat. A severe case may even reduce voice control to a squeak, often requiring the need for grunting or the making of other barely audible noises to reassure the afflictee that his/her speech box is still in working order.

Not everyone is susceptible to them, according to psychologist E.E. White of Ohio State University, but those who are can now take certain precautions to alleviate the full impact of their unceremonious assault. Dr. White suggests that victims who are unable, either by guile or direct falsehood, to avoid participating in stressful situations, should face the enemy unflinchingly. They should make up their minds to go through with it with the realization that they won't die from the experience.

Holding tightly to someone's hand or to an inanimate object may prevent an immediate collapse. However, a prolonged clutching only increases the anxiety of the ordeal and could even make it difficult to subsequently free oneself, thereby adding to the embarrassment of the moment and causing an audience to cackle with glee.

Dr. White explained that the best defense of all is calmness. "Develop an outward appearance of absolute control. Exude confidence in your surroundings and in yourself. Tell yourself that this time tomorrow it will all be over and you can relax with a very dry martini ⎯ hold the olive!

"Breathing is extremely critical," said Dr. White. "Rather than uttering subdued nervous sounds, breathing deeply and slowly will relieve tense muscles around the larynx and abdomen. It's the same principle practiced by professional athletes." Dr. White likened the example to a baseball pitcher who takes a deep breath when facing a batter on a three-two count. "It eases his nervousness and allows him to proceed confidently with the pitch."

There are worse ailments than the Nervous Nellies. Off-hand, none seem to come to mind, but a person continually tormented by them may take heart in knowing that these undesirable pests attack everyone sooner or later, and that the only certain defense against them lies in the subtle art of hara-kiri.

CHAPTER THIRTY-FIVE

Sometimes the simplest things can be the hardest to write about. Writing verses for children is a perfect illustration. Where adults can be influenced into their choice of literature by several ruses, not the least of which is false promise, children cannot be that easily swayed. A writer must be totally honest in capturing the fantasies of a child and that is not an easy task for grown up writers. We adults find it difficult to be a child again.

Children live in a world of imagination. They invent playmates that only they can see and hear and their young adventures take place within a sphere that few adults can enter. Robert Louis Stevenson was a notable exception. He was able to enter the world of children at will. His little verses were the key — verses such as "At The Sea-Side."

> "When I was down beside the sea
> A wooden spade they gave to me
> To dig the sandy shore.
>
> My holes were empty like a cup.
> In every hole the sea came up,
> Till it could come no more."

Stevenson wrote for older kids as well. "Treasure Island" has endured for more than a hundred years as the most popular of children's stories. He delighted in writing tales of youthful adventure and he, more than any other, is the standard by which authors of children's tales measure themselves.

Writers who wish to create poems and stories for children cannot write as if they are merely observers. They must themselves become as children in their thinking. They must experience the world surrounding them as would a child and select their words accordingly. Whether they succeed is reflected in the face of children.

Children are the best audience that a writer can find. My own grandchildren are often used as guinea pigs while I read them a short story. I watch their faces and solicit their questions to determine whether a particular story works or does not. People who succeed in reaching a ripe old age like to dispel their years by claiming they are still children on the inside. However, the older we get, the more difficult it is to recall our youthful imagination.

I particularly remember several occasions as a child when I was so sleepy that I left my shoes on the staircase to be found the next morning; and a poem was born.

>
> Two little shoes upon the stair,
> I wonder just who put you there,
> Did you climb all by yourselves,
> Or were you helped by little elves?
> Little shoes all ready for bed,
> Were you left behind by a sleepy head?

Although it was a faithful recollection, this poem is an example of having been created by an observer. It didn't pass the grandchildren test. "Goldfish Lost," however, was a different matter.

> Once I had a goldfish,
> Small as he could be.
> I rather liked his friendly ways
> And thought that he liked me.
>
> But one day while I changed his bath
> I cried when it was done

For no matter where I looked for him
I found that he was gone.

I searched inside his crystal bowl
But nowhere could I see
My little goldfish anywhere;
I asked, "Where can he be?"

I finally found my little friend
As snug as he could be
Swimming in his castle pool
And smiling up at me.

    My grandchildren also particularly enjoyed a little story in which I used their real names to tell about a sneaky snake that lived in a bramble bush. Devin and his two cousins, Sarah and Chrissy, were playing in the backyard and ignoring an earlier warning, they decided to look for that old snake. Devin and Sarah became stuck in the bramble bush and thought the snake had caught them while Crissy ran for help. The tale was apparently so vivid to Devin that he later cried and asked to be forgiven for having disobeyed his Grampa and getting stuck in the bramble bush. He now tells the story himself as if it actually happened. I felt like I found the key to his world.

    Charles Lutwidge Dodgson was another writer who found the key into the world of children. Under the pseudonym, Lewis Carroll, he wrote the stories published as "Alice's Adventures In Wonderland" which became widely read. He followed up with "Through The Looking Glass" and Alice was forever immortalized.

    Children know what they like and are quick to tell you what they don't like, although they may not be able to give you a reason for either.

CHAPTER THIRTY-SIX

Since the advent of the computer chip, there have been so many newfangled gadgets developed to make lives easier and less complicated for engineers, scientists, mechanics, teachers, generals and housewives; surely there must be something new for the writer.

I have in mind an electronic cliché remodeler. If a writer forgets and says that someone or something is snug as a bug in a rug, the CR will beep and alternatives immediately begin flashing

> "Snug as ? a bear in winter,
> ? honey in a hive,
> ? tick on a hound dog."

There is probably a great need for keyboard mufflers so early risers will not wake the rest of the household while hacking away on that manuscript. How about automatic coffee/donutters for the same people, or computerized sandwichers for those who feel compelled to work throughout the night? Perhaps there could be some kind of meter to measure the number of exclamation points or apostrophes as they are put into use. I'm sure writers could use a rejection analyzer to provide all the reasons that an editor might give for not publishing the work in progress.

Computers already provide spell checkers, thesauruses and grammar-looker-uppers so it should be relatively simple to devise some kind of program to create, fold, stamp and mail with little exertion on the part of a writer.

Writers are supposed to be inventive when it comes to new words. I am reminded of the cartoon showing two cavemen looking at the carvings on a wall and one says, "What do you mean it's misspelled? I just made it up." That caveman was one of the world's first writers but he certainly won't be the last to coin a new word. Some of us do it carelessly, others purposefully, but we all do it at one point or another.

Ogden Nash was perhaps the most inventive of all. Everyone is familiar with his humorous innovations, like "In the Vanities/ No one wears panities." He concocted other words and rhymes as it suited him. Such as "walcome" to rhyme with talcum, "torgia" to rhyme with Borgia, "thinked" for extinct, "parentical" with identical, and "kissome" to rhyme with lissome. In spite of his seeming mockery of the English language, he was by contrast also one of the most insightful of poets. I shall always be fond of one of his verses which ends . . .

"People watch with unshocked eyes;
But the old men know when an old man dies."

Subtle irreverence in the case of Ogden Nash should not be confused with disrespect, as might be the case with others who have the single intention of being spiteful or disparaging rather than humorous. A writer who employs the many avenues of humor does so to entertain and to amuse without being offensive.

The creation of new words occurs every day. Some fall by the wayside when they fail to capture the fancy of the average reader while a few progress into the acceptable arena of everyday usage. There is nothing improper about poets and writers using unknown words, unknown that is, until now. If a particular act or expression can be further explained by using an artistically inspired word, it is to a writer's advantage to do so. Chances are he won't be remembered for it even if the new word finds itself ensconced in Webster's dictionary, but if the writer fears to be daring, he too may fall by the wayside.

There was talk not long ago about a national Write-Off competition to determine the most talented of contemporary American poets. I don't know if such a thing will ever come to pass but if so I would like to suggest a few rules. First of all, no one under the age of thirty should be allowed to enter. That should just about eliminate the depressives, the hallucinatory, the militants and the near-suicides. It doesn't completely legitimize the remaining candidates but it does give the rest of us a more than average chance.

The second rule should require all poets to be published in journals other than those sponsored by University presses and certain literary journals. Call it sour grapes but I cannot help but believe there were better entries in the 1989 Slipstream contest than "The Fat Boy With No Imagination From Down The Block." For all his B.S. in English, his M.A. in Creative Writing, and his Ph.D., the author of that poem appeared to be a perfect example of those who propel readers away from poetry rather than endearing them. Who would knowingly seek such pretentious drivel except another pseudo-intellectual who writes only for other poets? Is it any wonder that poetry is in such dire straits with today's readers? How many entries in this particular contest selection will be remembered a hundred years from now, or fifty years, or even one year?

Aw hell! Maybe it is sour grapes.

Poetry contests are generally unrewarding since there are only one or two winners and the prizes seldom add food to the table. They do, however, present a real challenge because they provide a topic and a format, or at least a restrictive number of lines to work with. I rather enjoy participating in competitions for the opportunity provided to create poetry that I might not otherwise have attempted. Some of my best work resulted from creating within the guidelines of a contest. Poems often have a habit of writing themselves with little assistance beyond the actual typing and competitions give a starting point or a title theme. The poem proceeds from there.

The final rule should be an insistence that all poet candidates show proof of having read the works of five other contemporary poets. Poets may not be able to create a poem of such uniqueness that it offers a new discovery with each reading, but writing poetry can still be fun whether the writer is of school age or somewhat in the range of senior citizenship.

Regardless, poetry is for all ages.

It's fair to say that everyone has written a poem at one time or another; whether a simple Roses Red and Violets Blue verse reminiscent of youthful romanticists, or a scrapbook doodle selected for its relative ease in rhyming. A limerick is usually the second phase of development and may constitute an untested poet's first experience with alternate stress patterns. Limericks rival sonnets and epigrams in popularity and their creation is frequently eternally addictive in devising humorous situations presented in five anapestic lines.

The writing of poetry frequently begins with a feeling of enchantment for the arrangement of thoughts into metrical rhythm. This process eventually includes the use of syntax, illusion and much more, all of which act together to arouse literary passion. Neither the length of a poem nor its complexity is indicative of poetic value. Consequently, although poets strive for brevity they struggle in search of the precise word to make their poem work. A good poem must accomplish what its creator intended. It must arouse emotion, passion.

It is not from the old masters alone, however, that such poetry is created. Lesser known poets have similarly succeeded in accomplishing their personal goal. Perhaps they have learned that reading poetry is essential to writing it. This may be the greatest secret of all, for is there a better way of learning except to study what has gone before?

New poets possess an understandable urge to create and their desire is certainly whetted by something they have read. This is a learning experience and the ones who profit the most are those who absorb the fundamental elements of poetry. They are the learners who transpose the pleasures of reading into the exhilaration of writing, and who delight in the perfection of their craft.

Becoming a poet occurs at whatever age an individual is able to convey the imagery of thought into another person's mind, whether through the application of language or sound or visual impression.

Being a poet endures forever.

CHAPTER THIRTY-SEVEN

If your pen pal tells you that space aliens surreptitiously removed all traces of his (or her) latest book manuscript from the computer, do you (1) send your friend a sympathy card; (2) postpone any reply until your giggles subside; or (3) elicit more details because this sounds like the beginning of a good science fiction story?

A writer will invent all kinds of excuses as to why deadlines are missed or what happened to that promised magazine article. Those of us who live by the pen (so to speak) are often reluctant to explain our reasons for not following through on writing assignments even if the deadline is a self-imposed one.

"OK. I know I told myself that I could wrap up this travel feature in seven days but I haven't been feeling well and I can't really write anything when I'm feeling puny." Does that sound familiar?

More often than not, the truth lies somewhere between that old bugaboo writer's block and just pure old laziness. Some days we can't move ourselves to write another word. Either that or our muse decides to scamper off to wherever muses scamper, leaving us to fend for ourselves. I always blame things on my muse. The truth is I never knew I had a muse until I noticed a tendency to delay my writing from time to time. A muse is a handy body to have around.

Writers have struggled with this problem from the days of Og, the caveman. He too was forced to put down his chisel and finger-paints when his creative mood wore thin. Perhaps he felt a plaintive cry of protest for laboring long and hard to further the repute of his clan, or perhaps the tantalizing aroma of barbecued gnu interrupted his artistry in favor of the cooking fire.

It happens.

Many well-intentioned suggestions have been offered by seasoned writers to combat this momentary loss of the will to write. They have been there and should know whereof they speak, but is there really a panacea — a sure-fire remedy to cure this affliction? I think there is and it's a simple one. It is called a "manuscript in-progress file" and it works for me.

Keeping one's nose to the grindstone is a matter of always having some writing task to work on whenever the need arises for a change. Having alternative projects available helps to keep the juices flowing and the fingers typing. I maintain my in-progress file for such occasions. The advantage in this system lies in always having something else to work on whenever my interest wanes in a primary work project. I simply pull up my list of alternative manuscripts that were temporarily abandoned for various reasons and when I return to the primary writing project I often discover that the plot begins to flow smoothly once more.

Until the next time.

At present, I can count three unfinished fiction manuscripts, a serious novel, two magazine articles, a collection of poetry, and a high school research paper for my grandson, all standing by in case my muse takes leave. Meanwhile, my primary project is completed and mailed to an eagerly awaiting publisher. A new project is started immediately or I begin work on the next available in-progress project with scarcely a hitch.

Of course there is no real cure-all for intentionally putting off work that should be done. On the other hand, if a writer wants to lie around and soak up the tropical sun between manuscripts, that's different.

Keeping writers' noses to the grindstone is arguably the most difficult of all tasks but proper forethought can make it less of a problem than need be. It's a gimmick designed to keep the words appearing on a page and to achieve that byline and a check. Our first writing efforts are usually disastrous anyway and we develop different gimmicks along the way as we strive for literary success.

I first tried to write stories somewhere between the ages of three and thirteen. My parent's initial reaction to my effort was a scolding from mother and a spanking when father came home.

"You've got to do something about that child." My mother's words echo in my brain to this day as well as my dad's weary response, "what's he done this time?"

"He's been scribbling on the walls again."

If my parents had only been supportive during those formative years they might have been the hands to mold a future bestseller. They could have spawned a writer of note with nine initials following my name plus a summer home in Cannes and a university wing named in my honor.

Unfortunately, they not only failed to recognize the budding genius living under their roof but firmly rejected my youthful undertaking to establish the family fortune. They confiscated my crayons.

In spit of these hurdles, perseverance brought me to the brink of literary fame as a high school sophomore. I discovered H. G. Wells and my twig was bent. His fantasy journeys to the center of the earth, beneath the sea, and to the moon fueled my desire to create similar adventures. I gathered some highly imaginative characters together in a space ship and sent them off on an interplanetary voyage, complete with clashing meteorites, flashing sunspots, and dashing extraterrestrial beings. The entire ten-page manuscript was then trundled off to Amazing Stories Magazine and I settled back to wait for the check.

The next few weeks were filled with the thrill of anticipation. It was difficult keeping the impending news from my friends at school. I toyed with sharing my confident expectation with Honey Bun Singletary, the sweetheart of Herky High, but decided to wait until I could present her with the first autographed copy of my published story. My ego was walking six inches off the ground, and then the letter came.

I ripped it open being careful not to drop the enclosed check, but there was only the letter. "A good first effort," was all I could read before my eyes began losing focus. It isn't easy to see through salty tears as other writers have discovered. The publisher was kind enough to add a comment — "An interminable voyage without purpose" — and I had to admit he was right about that. I had been so caught up in the creation of personalities that I forgot about writing an inviting, credible story that readers would enjoy.

There have been other rejections, we all have them, but in their midst are also acceptances and a few awards trickling in. The tears no longer manifest themselves, outwardly at least, but I still hold my breath with the opening of each envelope bearing a publisher's return address, fearful of dropping an enclosed check.

Old habits are indeed hard to break.

CHAPTER THIRTY-EIGHT

Frustration causes much sighing and self-pitying plus a lot of lip pooching and some handwringing. I have never actually seen anyone wring their hands but I understand it's a widely known phenomena. Handwringing should not be confused with drywashing, kneading, or fingerpulling. These are legitimate human physical activities engaged in by folks in all walks of life, with the possible exception of fingerpulling for which crude old men are noted.

"Pull my finger, sonny." I believe that's how it goes.

There are times when hopes and aspirations fail to make it off the ground. Normal routines are often jostled and the rest of the day goes right down the drain. Then comes the sighing, the self-pitying, the lip pooching, and yes, the handwringing. Some folks seem more vulnerable than others to the frustrations of life. Who are they? Yep! You guessed it.

Writers, because of our sensitive nature, are among the foremost casualties in this group. Many of our writing frustrations are undoubtedly generated by ourselves. We labor for hours, days and longer, on stuff that we hope to sell. Unless we have effected a firm relationship with one particular editor, our stuff is often shunted around to various other editors until finally accepted or we run out of stamps. With each rejection, our lips begin to pooch more so we get busy and start more stuff winging its way to more editors. If we receive an acceptance, hopefully in the form of a check, the lip pooching is forestalled temporarily and we dive right in to work on more stuff.

There are other times when we suffer long periods of editorial rejection. Our stuff keeps returning in spite of constant polishing and self-editing. Publications that once featured our stuff close their doors and their erstwhile friendly editors disappear to wherever deposed editors go when they disappear.

"Hi! Welcome to the hinterlands. Do you have a reservation?"

"Yes I have. My name is Millard . . . Rayburn Millard. I'm an editor."

"I think you mean, you *were* an editor, Ha! Ha! A little hinterland humor there. Oh yes, we have a reservation in your name. Sort of a last minute thing, was it not!"

I suppose that such an occurrence would prove that editors are susceptible to frustrations the same as writers. In fact, it may be difficult to recognize that particularity in a few of them. Nonetheless, it's true. Writers who concede to an uncounted number of disappointments and hardships often infiltrate the enemy camp and become editors themselves. Not uncommon are those editors who maintain their writing status by continuing to produce a modicum of verse or prose under their own byline. Fortunately, they enjoy a close relationship with their publisher/employer

No one talks about manuscripts that fail to achieve publication. That's because they seemingly have died on the vine and are never heard from afterwards. They are neither reviewed nor excerpted and their author lives out his lonely life in seclusion and despair. It is the stuff of writers that fill unopened notebooks, memories that bring a teardrop to a cheek, and a bit of nostalgia for the words born of a writer's imagination.

Doctor's offices are brimming with patients afflicted with many different kinds of frustrations. Very few are writers, however, because writers generally do not seek professional help for something that happens more often than not. Our purse strings can't afford it in the first place and our egos won't permit it in the second place. In the third place, we prefer to endure silently and stoically until our previously rejected stuff becomes wanted by a new editor, someone obviously unaware of our literary reputation and in desperate need of a filler.

As writers, we must be ready when that happens. We must disregard the frustrations of the past and exchange the dust of our old stuff for the freshness of new stuff.

That's what writers do.

While researching for this book, I cautioned myself not to write about the usual things that frustrated writers write about. We all recognize the clichés that serve to clutter up articles with pointless advice such as "write only about things you know," or "be ready in case a bolt of lightning signals the birth of a new idea." There are others but I need not parade the do's and don'ts at this time. In fact, there are possibly less do's than there are don'ts when it comes to writing about writing. A good example is "don't complain that all the good ideas have already been taken and there is nothing left to write about. Our old friend Og probably used that particular excuse to explain his writer's block when it came time to decorate the new cave.

It's a courageous act to write about writing. Doing so falsely implies that the author professes to have more knowledge on the subject of writing than other writers. Regardless, the author does risk a certain amount of animosity among his peers for having the sheer audacity to attempt writing about writing.

"Who does this guy think he is?"

"What guy, Charlie?"

"The guy who wrote this piece about writing."

"What's wrong with it?"

"Well, I haven't read it yet but I probably know as much as he does."

It takes a lot of study and preparation to become an accomplished writer and writers are forever studying and practicing their craft. Successful novelists and essayists will be the first to admit that although their work may be widely published, they still try to make each new offering better than the previous one.

There is a distinct knack to writing about writing. It isn't crucial for a writer to be an expert in this field but it is an absolute necessity to analyze the subject thoroughly and to organize his/her presentation to achieve the greatest impact. Other writers will read what has been written and will fully expect to either learn something new or be entertained in the process. It has always been my fondest desire to be invisible just to observe the reactions of other writers as they scan my words and to see their heads nodding in agreement over something I've propounded, or even to snicker at a bit of silly nonsense from my pen.

The trick is not to write in a competitive mood but in a manner to suggest that all writers have suffered similar trials and indignities and can now laugh at themselves for wanting to be writers in the first place. It's unlikely that anything one writer has to say about writing will help anyone else become a better writer. New writers are constantly reading what others have to say when they should be doing the *only* thing that would really help them to improve their talents, and that is write, write, write.

Publication is the payoff for the long hours of labor that writers endure and a byline is the reward. Editors and publishers know what sells their product, whether poetry or fiction, and what genre of either their readers will support. Anything else is simply not considered for their publication. Contributors must therefore offer editors what they want if a byline is to be attained. There will be no changing of this system and fledgling writers would do well to remember it. However, this does not imply a complete unconditional surrender of the writer.

The spirit of Emily Dickinson is alive and well.

Writing without publication in mind is probably the "freest" free verse of this era. It is created without any constraint as to style, pattern or rhyme and is limited only by poetic imagination and inspiration. Emerson called it "poetry of the portfolio."

Because the writings are purely private and personal, the author is free to express daring and unconventional thoughts unaccompanied by the discipline of public criticism or conformity to editorial demands. It is a means of providing a venue for those poems or random ideas that occasionally spring up for no apparent reason and for which there is no selling market. They can now be encouraged to blossom without fear of being lost forever in the labyrinth of a poet's mind; and who knows, they may yet surface as "The Best of . . . "

The ideas behind the little verses and essays appearing on these pages were sort of borrowed from other poets, other writers of song, essayists, dramatists, novelists and journalists. Readers may discover traces of Buchwald, Teepen, Grizzard, Bombeck, Rooney, Fulghum, and Bly in some of the things I have written simply because their work has been the model of my personal admiration. But let me be quick to point out that I usually focused on one phrase or thought so as to change their various viewpoints to one of my own. I trust that my own viewpoints may have struck a fellow writer's funny bone now and then.

I also confess to shaking the proverbial literary tree for the source of many writing ideas. Such sources were more often the writers themselves rather than what they had written. William Shakespeare has always been a favorite target. His prolific sonnets and dramatic plays provided an everlasting avenue of material for my parodic brain. No attempt was made to dispute his reputation as an accomplished actor best known for having produced an estimated thirty-eight plays and 154 sonnets; although, a controversy yet rages over whether he actually wrote all of those sonnets.

Emily Dickinson's self imposed privacy has piqued my satirical side as has the works, the loves, and the lives of Robert Burns, Percy Shelley, Carl Sandburg, Edgar Allan Poe; the list goes on and on. Readers should take particular note that all my targeted literary prey are no longer among the living. This fact allows me the freedom to jab at them in fun and even to besmirch them on occasion in a humorous vein. I can do this because they're all dead and gone and cannot avenge themselves. Or can they? Now, there's another possible essay idea.

I am trying to say that writing about writing doesn't have to be boring or purely instructional. It can be entertaining and fun to read if it is also fun to write, and that pretty much sums up my philosophy on writing.

- o -

AUTHOR'S BIO

Thomas Edward Lynn was born in 1930 at St. Louis, Missouri. A professional law enforcement officer, he taught report writing courses at the Federal Law Enforcement Training Center at Glyncoe, Georgia.

A soldier, poet, husband, father and grandfather, he has also been a regular contributing editor for Writers Rescue Magazine and a columnist for Sharing & Caring Magazine. His fiction bylines include *The Last Battle* published by Sandpiper Press and *Gurney's Squad* published in Sharing & Caring. Lynn's essays and articles have been published in Army Magazine, Writer's Journal, Writer's Guidelines & News and Mediphors. He is a member of the Georgia Poetry Society, the Georgia Writers Inc., and the Gulf Coast Writers Association.

In 1995, his poem *Old Comrades* was engraved on a Korean War Memorial monument and unveiled at the Mount Hope Cemetery in Bangor, Maine.